6-30-19

TeresA, I hope
you will enjoy Our
Story. IT was a
fun remembering all
good Times we had as young "

God BLess,

Jon

The *Memories*

A Doo-Wop Journey

Lou Martin

CROSSBOOKS
PUBLISHING

CrossBooks™
A Division of LifeWay
1663 Liberty Drive
Bloomington, IN 47403
www.crossbooks.com
Phone: 1-866-879-0502

First published by CrossBooks 09/13/2012

ISBN: 978-1-4627-2122-1 (sc)
ISBN: 978-1-4627-2121-4 (e)
ISBN: 978-1-4627-2120-7 (hc)

Library of Congress Control Number: 2012916435

Printed in the United States of America

This book is printed on acid-free paper.

Contents

Foreword

For a long time, I've thought of writing about my professional singing career in a vocal group with four teenage guys from southeast Washington, DC. I finally decided that if I was ever going to write anything of substance about my fifty-five years performing with the Bobolinks and the Memories, then I had better get started. The clock is ticking!

When I began my research for this book, I had absolutely no idea what writing a book entailed. I originally thought it would be easy because of my professional background as a police officer; congressional investigator; published poet, singer, and song writer. Even with my work history, I was totally unprepared for what I was about to experience. What an eye-opening experience it turned out to be.

We have all heard the story about an experiment where one person from a group tells another person a set of facts. That person then turns to a third person and passes on the same information. This person then passes the information to a fourth party, and so on, until the last person to get the information shares the facts he or she received with the rest of the group. What comes out is a story that is almost unrecognizable when compared to the original story. I ran into exactly this type of situation while researching the history of the Bobolinks and the Memories.

Many individuals who have interacted with the Memories during our fifty-six years together had lots of stories to share about our group's history. A good portion of the information received from those well intentioned people unfortunately proved to be contradictory, and in a few cases, downright wrong. I understand that this is not unusual when writing about people's memory of past events that occurred many years ago. While researching this story, even my own memory of certain events proved fuzzy, and I was there.

This book contains the best information I could gather about a group of teenage boys who during their musical journey made many mistakes, but also forged lifelong friendships in the pursuit of a shared dream. During their journey, they also proved they had the talent, and more importantly, the tenacity to make it in show business. I have attempted to show how perseverance and plan old stubbornness paid off in the later years with success and peer recognition for the Memories. I encountered some gaps in our group's history that despite a large amount of research, I was unable to fill. This is not due to any lack of effort on my part, but more to fading memories and the passage of time. I hope you enjoy this book.

— Louis Martin

Acknowledgments

To Ronnie Lutz, for the use of your remarkable memory throughout this project and for your unwavering friendship during this long journey we have taken together.

To Robert "Boots" Dove, for your input and support for this project of mine, and for your friendship over these more than fifty-five years. I miss you.

To Glenn Bortz, a talented musician who has been solid as a rock for the Memories and who helped to make us better. A real professional and friend!

To the original members of the Bobolinks: Jimmy Durst, Gene Fitzgerald, Boots Dove, Ronnie Lutz, and myself, forerunners of the present-day Memories. We shared a dream.

To the rest of the Memories remarkably talented musical family, who have helped make us the success we have become: Robert Dove Jr., Charlie Helmick, Mike Scheer, Rick Williamson, and our newest member, June Flynn. You are all truly amazing people.

To Buddy Catzva, a man with a vision, who helped guide a band of rowdy teenagers toward the realization of their dream. He will forever be remembered for being a major part of our history. What a guy!

To all those musicians and singers, who were once a proud part of the Memories musical family and whose names now reside on the Memories Wall of Honor, I salute you.

To all the group member's wives, Sandy Martin, Ginny Lutz, Patty Bortz, Pam Helmick, Marge Scheer, and Linda Williamson, thank you for your love and unselfish support over these many years helping us live our dream. To our loyal road crew, George and Judy Shaffier, we will never be able to thank you enough.

To the untold number of our fans who throughout the years have shown their loyalty and support by following our musical path and by buying the records, albums, and tickets that made it all possible. You have our undying gratitude.

Chapter 1

The Beginning of My Musical Career: I Meet the Bobolinks

In the summer of 1957, I had just graduated from Eastern High School with high hopes and a lot of time on my hands. Like most young guys my age I was looking for something to do before going back to school in the fall. One of my close friends, Wayne Bramble, was really into current music and the latest top forty songs. One day he approached me and asked if I would go with him to hear a singing group that he thought was outstanding. He said the group was from the Anacostia area of southeast Washington, DC, and the group would be performing at a club in nearby Waldorf, Maryland, called the Lamplighter Club. I agreed to go with him later that evening.

Wayne and I took off for the Lamplighter Club at about six o'clock. At that time, both Wayne and I lived in southeast Washington, DC, and Waldorf, Maryland was way out in the suburbs or so it seemed to us then. When we pulled up to the club after a thirty-five minute drive, the place looked like a dump from the outside. After we went inside, I was proven right. The place was run down; it was small inside with a tiny dance floor and stage. When we entered the club, Wayne waved to a couple of guys whom I didn't know that were sitting in a booth by the stage. We had just sat down in a separate booth when the two guys he had previously waved to came over. Wayne introduced them to me as members of the

Bobolinks, the group we had come to see. I really don't remember which two they were, but a few minutes later when they began to sing, I knew that I really wanted to get to know them and become a part of the group. Their harmony was absolutely the best I had ever heard up to then, and right then I started plotting how I would become a part of the group. Many years later, I learned that the Bobolinks had earned the princely sum of $15 for their night's performance at the club.

About a week later, I spoke with Wayne and asked him how I could get in touch with the guys in the Bobolinks. He told me that they usually hung out at a place in the Anacostia area called the Hi Ho, and I could probably catch some of them there in the afternoons after school. I asked Wayne to go with me to the Hi Ho later that week to meet the guys and hopefully get an invitation to join the group .He agreed to come with me to meet the guys, which made me feel a lot better about my first meeting with them. I didn't know if they were even interested in adding any new members to the group at that time, but I knew I had to give it a try. I really wanted to sing with them.

On Wednesday of that same week, Wayne and I went to the Hi Ho. My heart was beating really fast when we first entered the restaurant. It was right after the local high schools, Anacostia High and Kramer Jr. High, had let out for the day, and the Hi Ho was jammed with kids yelling orders to the guys working behind the counter. It was controlled chaos. I remember thinking many years later that the Hi Ho really was a real life version of the TV show *Happy Days* many years before that show ever appeared on TV.

Despite all the confusion of the kids yelling out orders to the soda jerks (one of whom, Gabe Fleri, would later become a dear friend), the jukebox playing, and high school kids just being kids, Wayne managed to get me to the end of the counter and introduce me to the owner of the Hi Ho, Buddy Catzva. Buddy turned out to be not only the owner of the Hi Ho restaurant, but he also was one of the nicest guys I've ever met.

The first thing he said to me was "I bet you've never had a milkshake like mine before." I could only shake my head no, because I hadn't been there before and had never tasted his shakes. He asked me what my favorite ice cream was and I told him chocolate. He proceeded to make me the best milkshake I had ever tasted. As soon as I started to drink the shake, he asked me if I wanted to be one of the Bobolinks. I nodded yes, and he said that he would get Jimmy over to talk to me in a few minutes. I figured out later that Wayne had already spoken to them about my desire to join the group.

After a few minutes had passed, Jimmy Durst made his way over to Wayne and me, shook my hand, and introduced himself. Jimmy said that he understood that I was interested in getting into the group and wanted to know which harmony part I sang. I really didn't know at the time because I fancied myself as a lead singer and knew very little about singing harmony. Boy was I in for a surprise. Jimmy said not to worry about it; they would figure it out later. He then invited me to his house the following afternoon to meet the rest of the group and his mother.

Chapter 2

I Audition for the Bobolinks

On the next day, I was very nervous about meeting the rest of the guys at Jimmy's house because I personally didn't know any of them, and Wayne had also told me that Jimmy's mother was a tough old lady who wouldn't put up with any nonsense. When I pulled up in front of Jimmy's house at Sixteenth and S streets, SE, that afternoon, I was sweating bullets. My desire to join the group overcame my fear, and I walked up to the house. Jimmy greeted me at the front door; right behind him stood an older woman and a young girl. Jimmy introduced them to me as his mother and his sister Susanne. His mother invited me in and immediately asked if I wanted to be in the group, and if so, what song I wanted to sing for my audition. I was totally unprepared, and I had no idea that I would have to audition for this group, much less have a song ready to sing. Boy was I full of myself! I stuttered and stammered a bit, but I finally came up with a song, "In the Still of the Night" by the Five Satins that was very popular at the time. Mrs. Durst told me to go into the living room where Susanne was waiting in front of a beautiful baby grand piano. She looked at me and asked what key I sang the song in, which caught me off guard. I had no idea what key I sang the song in, because up to that point, I just sang along with the record when I heard it played on the radio or jukebox.

Jimmy's sister surprised me when she said, "Don't worry about it; just sing a few bars and I'll get the key." I started singing, and she quickly stopped me and said, "It's in the key of F." She then started playing the song and I started singing. Finally, after what seemed to me like a very long time, the song ended, and his mother looked at me, pointed toward the basement door and said, "You'll do just fine. Go on down to the basement; they're waiting on you."

I was so relieved and happy to be done with the audition. Had I known beforehand that Herb Feemster of the future hit duo, Peaches and Herb, had auditioned for the group earlier, I would've been a basket case. I later learned from Jimmy that Herb had not been accepted into the group at the time. Anyway, I was feeling very happy about my audition, and I almost ran down the stairs to the basement.

In the basement, Jimmy introduced me to the other guys in the group, Gene Fitzgerald, Robert "Boots" Dove, and Ronnie Lutz. All the guys, with the exception of Ronnie Lutz, greeted me warmly and welcomed me to the group. Being the new guy, I didn't know the dynamics of the group makeup or its internal politics. I was about to find out the hard way.

After meeting everyone in the group, we started to discuss the vocal arrangements of the different songs they had been practicing before I joined the group. Jimmy wanted me to sing lead on a few songs that Ronnie had been singing lead, which explained Ronnie's cool reception toward me. I also knew that even though Jimmy had explained to Ronnie that my voice was a higher tenor and better suited to those particular lead vocals, our relationship would still be cool. Ronnie was a fiery redhead with a temper. Without going on too much about my relationship with Ronnie, we butted heads for quite some time before we settled into what could be called, more or less, a truce. Over the years, our friendship would mature and deepen to the point where we became best friends.

Chapter 3

Jerry Toronto

After joining the group, Ronnie and Jimmy told me about some of the people who had played a part in helping the group develop during the very beginning of the Bobolinks. . One was a local man named Jerry Toronto, who became sort of a manager and booking agent for our group. In reality, he was our first so-called manager. He was a really nice guy, who acquired a lot of work for the Bobolinks with the USO organization, which enabled us to perform for military personnel at numerous military bases around the country. He also entered our group in numerous talent contests throughout the Mid-Atlantic region, and at local clubs such as Stricks, and the Victory Grill. Occasionally, Jerry would also MC the various talent contest in which we performed, even though he had a vested interest in the outcome. The good thing was that the audience ultimately decided who won. We always did, and our guys honestly felt that we deserved to win. We were still full of ourselves.

Chapter 4

Gene Winters WPGC Radio

Our second so-called manager, Gene Winters, was another local guy who happened to be an extremely popular disc jockey with one of Washington, DC's hottest top forty radio stations, WPGC. Almost all the white teenagers in the DC area during the mid to late fifties listened to WPGC. Gene tried really hard to help our group, even helping us record a demo of our song "I Promise," but he was so deeply involved with his own career, as well as coping with the payola scandal going on in the radio industry at that time, that he didn't have much time to help promote a local teenage singing group. Several months later, we parted company with Gene, remained friends, and stayed in touch with him for several years thereafter. We were all hugely disappointed. Even though we were upset, we continued with our dream of making it in show business.

Chapter 5

WEAM Radio and Colt 45 Records

Things always seemed to be happening on the local music scene for our group. During the late 1950s (1958–59) we had the good fortune with the help of another local disc jockey, Jay Perry of WEAM Radio, to enter more than twenty-three local talent contests, in such locations as the Alpine Room, Stricks, Victory Grill, the Hyattsville Armory, and Sardo Hall, to name just a few. We won them all, and we were so full of ourselves.

Jay also introduced us to Ted Pettis, who with his brother owned the circle theater in downtown Washington, DC, along with the Circle Recording Studio. More importantly, we found out they owned Colt 45 Records, a record company that was well known in the recording industry for finding and recording hit artists. After hearing the Bobolinks sing, the Pettis brothers were so impressed with us that they attempted to sign our group to a contract on the spot. We were all for it, but because some of us were under the legal age to enter into a contract, they had to approach our parents to co-sign the recording contract. At that moment in time (July, 1959) with help from the Pettis brothers, we felt that we were on the verge of really making it big. We eventually recorded a couple of records for Colt 45 Records, but from that point, our relationship with Ted seemed to fizzle. When our contract with Colt 45 Records expired, it was not renewed. It was a huge letdown for all of us, and we were heartbroken, but it proved to be an incentive for us to just work harder. It was just another heartbreak we had to overcome. We were not going to quit!

8

Chapter 6

The Milt Grant TV Show

In 1958, before our third manager Buddy Catzva came on the scene, the Bobolinks entered a talent contest for WTTG Channel 5 TV in Washington, DC. Milt Grant was the show's host. Milt originally came to the DC area in the early fifties, where he worked at several radio stations such as, WINX, WWDC, and WOL, before he approached WTTG in 1956 with his idea for a teen dance show. WTTG bought his idea, and the *Milt Grant Record Hop* began in September, 1956. The original show only aired on Saturday afternoons between four and five o'clock. In 1957, the show changed names to *The Milt Grant Show* and began to air every Monday through Friday from five to six o'clock. The show became a wildly successful teen dance show that most of the teenagers in the greater Washington area knew about and watched. The show aired in an after-school time slot that almost guaranteed it to be a hit.

The Bobolinks not only won the talent contest, but the prize was also an invitation to perform live on the show. Almost all the television shows aired back then, were broadcast live. As a result, we practiced very hard to get our songs down pat. The Milt Grant Show show was produced and aired from the top floor of the Raleigh Hotel in downtown Washington, DC. When we arrived at the hotel to do our show, we went straight to the bathroom down the hall from the studio to again rehearse our songs. The bathroom was tiled and had a great echo to it, which made us sound great. At this point in time, our group didn't have the final vocal lineup

Lou Martin

we had hoped for, but we continued to perform, while actively searching for people that would fit our group's vocal requirements.

The group that showed up for *The Milt Grant Show* performance included Billy Suddith and Larry Lawrensen, both of whom had a tendency to sing the same harmony note. When we went into the studio to perform, the room where the show was broadcast seemed very small to us. We had all watched the show on television many times, and from what we had seen on TV, the studio appeared to be very big. The room was full of teenagers, along with two big television cameras on wheels being moved around the studio by cameramen. Milt Grant was just finishing a commercial about Tops Drive Ins and was holding a hamburger in his hand, talking about the Tops secret sauce that made the hamburger special. He looked kind of dorky, and he wore heavy makeup for the cameras, which made the whole thing seem kind of fake to me. During the next decade, Milt Grant went on to become very rich and successful in the cable TV industry, and he founded television's Channel 20 in 1966. Not so dorky, huh!

About this time, one of the studio staff told us to get ready to sing immediately after the commercial ended and to watch for his signal to start our song. Talk about nervous! When he gave us the signal, we began to sing "The Japanese Sandman," a song that was popular at the time. Both Billy and Larry sang the same note during the song, but we got through it, and we received a lot of enthusiastic applause from the kids in the studio. The show received so much good feedback from the viewers that Milt Grant invited us back to do additional TV shows for him. He also had the Memories perform for him at the Hyattsville Armory for his record hop shows. After our performances on TV, we became neighborhood celebrities, and we had lots of people trying to get us to perform for their organizations. Sadly, Milt's last TV show was broadcast in April, 1961. Things were beginning to change.

After our performances, our popularity skyrocketed, and we continued to be very busy, performing in several states that received *The Milt Grant Show.* . The group even found the time to meet and rehearse two or three evenings a week. We met at both Jimmy and Ronnie's house's, depending on various family concerns at the time. By that I mean, both Jimmy and Ronnie had married, and meeting and practicing at their houses was not always practical because of family considerations. Both of their wives may have been less than enthusiastic about our singing group for a variety of reasons—one of those reasons was that we performed for, and were exposed to, a lot of teenage girls. Just saying!

Chapter 7

We Lose Gene

*L*ess than a year after I joined the group and much to my surprise and disappointment, Gene Fitzgerald, who I thought was a terrific first tenor and an important part of the original Bobolinks harmony, decided to leave the group. He explained to us that being in the group was causing problems with his marriage, and he felt his marriage was more important. I was sorry to see him leave the group. We were all very angry with his wife Peggy, and we blamed his leaving on her. We were all very selfish at the time. We thought the world revolved around our singing group, so naturally we wouldn't believe we were in any way responsible for his marital problems. As time passed, I personally became a lot less selfish in the way I viewed his leaving the group, and I began to understand and appreciate both his and his wife's point of view. To this day, I retain my friendship with Gene, and I occasionally touch base with him.

Chapter 8

Herb Feemster

H erb Feemster used to meet with our group a lot during the summer months of 1957 at a park area called Fairlawn, near the Sousa Bridge in southeast Washington DC where we hung out and practiced singing together. Herb was a really nice guy, with a big smile and a very good voice. Many years later, he achieved great musical success with the singing duo, Peaches and Herb. Although the guys in our group consider him a friend, we have not seen him much over the years. After that summer in 1957, we never had the opportunity to sing together again. Both Herb and I later became members of the Metropolitan Police Department of Washington, DC, but we never had the opportunity to work together while on the job.

Chapter 9

Buddy Catzva and the Hi Ho Restaurant

Buddy Catzva became our group manager. He occasionally asked the guys in the group to help out behind the counter at the Hi Ho during the after-school hours when lots of local school kids came pouring in for burgers and shakes. When more than a couple of our group members were present, we occasionally sang a few well-known hit songs for the kids, while also helping to fill food orders for the customers. Buddy also knew and overlooked the fact that the Bobolinks consumed a lot of those food orders. He also noticed that his supply of chocolate ice cream was running out a lot quicker than usual, now that I was with the group. Buddy always seemed to know everything we were up to, but we all knew how much he and his beautiful wife, Ruth, loved us all. They were the ones who worked to keep a bunch of wild and crazy teenagers out of trouble and staying focused on reaching for our dream.

Speaking of Buddy and Ruth, I have to tell the story about the two of them taking one of their very few vacations away from the Hi Ho. Buddy came to us one evening while we were practicing in the backroom of the Hi Ho. He asked us if we would be willing to help paint the interior walls of the Hi Ho while he and Ruth went to Atlantic City for the weekend. He offered to pay us for our time, and he told us he would provide all the paintbrushes and paint needed for the job. We all agreed to help with the painting and skip any payment.

Buddy and Ruth left for Atlantic City, and all the group members met the following day at the Hi Ho, which was a Saturday, and began to get ready to start painting. After painting for a very short time, we decided to stop and take a short snack break. That short break turned into a full afternoon of singing, goofing off, and eating almost all of Buddy's supply of burgers, hot dogs, and ice cream. That's not to say that we didn't attempt to paint a little more of the restaurant walls, which we did, but we just didn't get much of the job done before Buddy and Ruth returned. We, as a group, felt a little bit guilty, and we decided to confess to Buddy about the missing food. To his credit, Buddy never raised hell with us about it, but he did say, in the future, he would get professional help when contemplating having any work done at the Hi Ho. He also expressed his curiosity about how so few guys could have consumed so much food and ice cream over such a short time span. He was laughing when he said it. What a guy!

During the next few months, the group rehearsed almost every evening at the Hi Ho or at Jimmy's house in the Southlawn section of Prince George's County, Maryland. Our voices really started to blend, and we became so attuned to one another's singing ability that we could switch harmony parts with one another when one of us snapped our fingers and keep on singing without missing a beat. While I continued to learn my harmony parts, we also continued to sing for the kids at the Hi Ho. As I mentioned at the beginning of this narrative, my memory, like most people's, is not the best when it comes to remembering various incidents in my life that occurred many years ago. To his credit, my friend Ronnie Lutz was a big help with putting the Bobolinks/Memories history into some sense of chronological order, so a few parts of my story will have benefitted from Ronnie's memory of specific group incidents in the past.

Chapter 10

Buddy Names His Restaurant

In late 1959, Buddy decided that we were ready to go into the studio to record a couple of records. He chose Edgewood Recording Studios, which was located on Sixteenth Street NW in Washington, DC. He chose Edgewood Studios because of their good reputation, equipment, and the studio's association with Columbia Records.

We began to practice six or seven nights a week for several weeks to get ready to record. Buddy chose two songs for us to record, "Mr. Frog" and "I Promise." We never really understood why Buddy picked "Mr. Frog" to record, but we recorded it. He also chose the name, Hi Ho, for his record label after the name of his restaurant (no surprise there!). How Buddy gave the name Hi Ho to both his restaurant and record company is an interesting story.

Buddy, in his youth, had been a professional boxer. As a result of boxing and participating in other sports, he damaged his knee. While in the hospital recovering from knee surgery, his roommate, who was an avid fan of anything Disney related, continuously played the theme song from the movie *Snow White and the Seven Dwarfs* on a portable 45 rpm record player. Buddy, until his surgery, hadn't picked a name for his new restaurant. After hearing "Hi ho, hi ho, it's off to work I go," played over and over for several hours, he decided it must be fate, and he named his restaurant the Hi Ho..

Chapter 11

Recording with the Legendary Sonny Stitt

When the big day arrived, we went downtown to the studio and were shown into the recording studio. Man, this whole recording experience was some heady stuff for a bunch of southeast boys to take in all at once. Here we were once again in a professional recording studio, getting ready to record our first professional recordings for Hi Ho Record Co. Jimmy Durst had brought his electric piano with him, and he began to set it up in the studio for our session. I was standing with Buddy by the door to our studio when three black guys who were in the hallway by our studio walked up to us and said, "You guys recording today?" We said yes, and one of them said, "Where's your horn player?" Buddy replied, "We don't have one." This same guy said, "Want us to sit in and help out?" Both Buddy and I wholeheartedly responded yes.

Both he and his friends went into the studio and began to prepare their instruments for our recording session. Wow! Now we had a saxophone player, a piano player, and drummer to help us. All three of them began to warm up, and after a few minutes of playing their instruments, the sax man turned to Buddy and said, "Let's give it a shot." Buddy then signaled the recording engineer behind the glass partition to let him know we were ready for a take, and then he left the studio. A take simply means that the recording artist is ready to begin the actual recording session.

Our group had already warmed up a few minutes earlier by rehearsing the two songs we wanted to record, so when the musicians indicated they were ready; we were all set to go. The music started, and we began to sing. Being surrounded by all that music was really nice because up until right then, we never had the experience of having a professional saxophone player and drummer play for us.

Chapter 12

What I Like Don't Sell

We finished "I Promise" and I felt that it was a pretty good take. The sax guy turned to us and said, "Let's do another take!" We agreed and did the song again, and everyone thought that it turned out a lot better than the first one. We next recorded "Mr. Frog." That song also turned out pretty good, although I've never really liked it much. After we finished the session, I approached the sax player who had so graciously helped us with our recording session and asked him, "Well, how did you like it?" What he said to me, I never really understood until many years later. He said, "Son, what I like don't sell, so you'll have to ask someone else that question."

I found out from Buddy many years later that the musician who played saxophone for us on that session was none other than the world famous Jazz saxophonist, Sonny Stitt. Only then did I realize what he had been talking about when he told me "What I like don't sell." I wish we had known at the time who the saxophone man was so we could have thanked him for being so kind toward a group of young singers. Buddy later told me that none of those gentlemen would accept any money from him for doing the session with us. How fine is that!

Chapter 13

Our First Suits

Another funny story about Buddy began with a phone call from Buddy to all the guys in the group, requesting us to come down to the Hi Ho for a meeting. Buddy wouldn't say what the meeting was about, which made us all wonder what was going on. Though we knew nothing about it at the time, this particular meeting resulted in the Bobolinks getting our first stage outfits. After we had all finally arrived, Buddy brought out these badly faded pink suits and proudly stated that he had purchased them from Morton's Department Store in Anacostia for ten dollars apiece.

He said he was able to get them at that great price because they had faded while on display in the window at Morton's. We all began laughing, and Buddy said, "Don't laugh, after I get them dyed, you'll love them." Well, to his credit, after the suits were dyed, they did look a lot better, but we never really liked them, and we only used them for a short time. None of us guys ever told anyone about the suits or how they had been acquired. You have to realize that we were all young men at the time and very much afraid of our group image suffering if the word got out about our ten-dollar pink suits from Morton's Department Store. Talk about peer pressure!

Chapter 14

Buddy Makes It Right

Buddy knew that we were embarrassed about wearing the suits he picked up from Morton's for ten bucks apiece. We had never said anything to him about the suits, because we all thought the world of both Buddy and Ruth, and we would never do anything to hurt their feelings. Buddy had decided that he would make amends to his "boys" and make things right. All of this took place without any of us in the group knowing anything about what Buddy intended to do.

I remember that a couple of months later Buddy called us all and told us to meet him at a downtown address the following day. Everyone wondered what Buddy was up too, and the next day we all hopped in Ronnie's car and drove to downtown Washington DC to meet him. We had theories about why he wanted us to come all the way downtown to meet him, but it remained a mystery until we arrived at the meeting spot.

When we arrived, we spotted Buddy waiting in front of a clothing store window. Being the geniuses that we were, we still didn't put two and together. We saw that he had a big grin on his face. One of us asked him "what's up, and Buddy pointed to the sign over the shop door and said, "This is the place where you get your real suits." We looked up and saw a sign over the door that read, Hong Kong Tailors.

We were still a little confused, but we all followed him into the store, where a small Asian gentleman greeted us and asked us to follow him. We proceeded to the back of the store, where Buddy told us that we were all going to be fitted for custom tailor-made suits. None of us had ever owned a tailor-made suit before, and most of us didn't even have an off-the-rack suit. We were all pretty excited and figured the worst that could come from this adventure was that we would each get a new suit.

The tailor measured us all from top to bottom. For the most part, the experience proved slightly uncomfortable, having a man put his hand up to your groin area, even while holding a tape measure, was disconcerting. We made it through the process, which turned out to be a learning experience. We also had a lot of fun. A few weeks later we picked up our suits, and they turned out beautifully. They were dark pinstriped suits with the Italian flap in the back, and the pants were slightly flared at the bottom. The suits even had our names embroidered on the inside jacket pocket. Talk about feeling special! Buddy had made things right in a big way. We were all so self-engrossed at the time that we never gave a thought to how much money Buddy must have spent. This was just one more way how both Buddy and Ruth showed their love for "their boys." Buddy was just that kind of man.

Chapter 15

Our First Musician: Dick Grimes

In the late fifties and early sixties we continued to rehearse and perform all over Washington, DC, at teen clubs and dances. Most of our performances during the early years of our group history were performed with almost no musical instruments. Except for Dick Grimes playing guitar, we didn't have any musicians helping us at the time. Although Dick was in reality the first guitar player to play with us for any length of time, the Bobolinks actually worked with another talented musician named Rudy Bautista, who was the first guitar player to appear in public with our group. Rudy only played for us once, at a popular Congress Heights Playground teen club dance. At that point in time, Congress Heights was a nice, safe area in southeast Washington, DC, Rudy resurfaced various times in the later years, to again play lead guitar for the Bobolinks/Memories.

Dickie, as we called Dick, had just left another local group, the Thunderbirds, when we first met him. I remember he once took us to a Thunderbirds rehearsal, and we were all excited about it until we got there. When we arrived at the location where the band was rehearsing, we quickly realized the band was playing so loud that we couldn't even hear ourselves sing. At the time, because of our collective naiveté, we considered the Thunderbird's to be professional musicians and looked up to them as someone to emulate. What a bummer for us.

Dick was a real character, and he used to give us hell about going off key when singing. When we would finish a song, he would give us a nasty look and then play a chord on his guitar and say, "This is where you started the song," and then he would play a different chord and say, "This is where you ended up. You're flat!" Dick didn't stay with us for any length of time, although he did record several demo records with us. Once, after recording a song with Dick in the studio, we were all standing around waiting for the engineer to play back the results. The engineer eventually played our recording back to us, and we began to hear a hollow ringing sound, which seemed to be in time with the beat of the record. We all tried unsuccessfully to figure out just where that sound was coming from. The recording engineer checked his equipment, but he couldn't find anything wrong. We all left the studio pretty bummed, because other than that annoying sound, the song came out pretty good.

Several days later, we finally figured out that the sound had come from Dick tapping his foot on the base of his microphone stand. I still have a copy of that recording. Dick eventually left our group to take a job with Safeway Food Stores as a butcher. We like to think that he left the group for a good paying job and not because he was disgusted with us for not staying on key. By the way, many years later, he retired from Safeway and became a successful charter boat captain in Deale, Maryland. I wonder if he still plays his guitar. I think the next time I see him, I'll ask that question. We remain friends with Dick to this day, and from time to time, we see him going back and forth to his charter fishing boat.

Chapter 16

Incident at Guam Hall

From 1958–1961, the Bobolinks were busy performing all around the metropolitan area at venues, such as Sardo Hall, Guam Hall, Mama Belosi's, and most of the volunteer fire departments and teen clubs scattered around the metro area. Factor in our group still singing at the Hi Ho a couple of times a week, along with appearing at local parties, and we stayed pretty busy.

In particular, I remember one night at Guam Hall, a public hall in the Anacostia section of southeast Washington, DC, when I acquired a fat lip just before I was scheduled to perform. My brother, Denny, who many years later became a singer with the Memories, was dating a girl from his school who unfortunately was also dating another guy from the same school. The inevitable happened, and they began to exchange threats and insults over this relationship. I heard through the grapevine that this other suitor had involved his older brother in the dispute, and the older brother had then threatened to kick Denny's butt.

At that time, my family was comprised of seven brothers and one sister. All the boys in our family had a reputation as being quick to fight if bothered and of not allowing anyone to intimidate or hurt one of our own. Most of the guys in our area knew not to mess with the Martin boys. We weren't necessarily the toughest guys around, but everyone knew that if you fought one of us, you had to fight us all. Because of family pride, I felt that I couldn't allow this threat to my brother to continue without some sort of response. I sent word to the older brother of Denny's rival to stay out of it and let them settle the problem between themselves. I should've taken my own advice.

A couple of weeks passed, and I thought the matter had been resolved. Oh, how wrong I was! The next Saturday night, I was with our singing group at Guam Hall, preparing for our performance. We were all in a small dressing room adjacent to the dance floor, when someone knocked on the dressing room door. I opened the door and saw two guys standing there. The guy in front said, "Are you Lou Martin?" I said yes. . He suddenly punched me in my face, and the fight was on. Never mind that I didn't know who this guy was or why he had hit me, I just began to try and protect myself from this assault.

Another interesting fact about this situation was at the time, I was a newly sworn member of the Metropolitan Police Department. So here I am, a cop, fighting with someone I didn't know over something I knew nothing about and not enjoying it one bit. I became really angry! As it turned out, I was a little better with my fists than the nameless person who had assaulted me. I'll give him credit; he tried hard to follow up on his first punch, but he picked the wrong guy to start a fight with. I seriously kicked his butt and then dragged him by his shirt across the crowded dance floor, with loud applause from the crowd, down the front steps of the building and over to a police call box (our department didn't have portable radios back then) where I called for a transport (a police paddy wagon) to come and pick him up. While waiting for the paddy wagon to arrive, I spoke with the guy and found out that he was the older brother of Denny's rival and also the same guy who had threatened him. I charged him with disorderly conduct, and the following day when I called the eleventh precinct to check on him, I was told he had paid his fine and was released from jail. I never heard from him again. Even though my assailant was gone, my problems were not entirely over. I returned to Guam Hall and went to the bathroom to inspect my face. I looked in the mirror and saw that my mouth was badly swollen, and I was talking funny. In retrospect, I think I looked pretty funny. Anyway, I went onstage despite my swollen lip sticking out what felt like a couple of inches. Even though singing hurt, we got through the evening's performance. What was the moral of this story? Don't get involved in teenage romantic squabbles, and more importantly, don't get sucker punched.

Chapter 17

Way-Lin Records and "Love Bells"

Nothing was more significant to the Memories/Bobolinks history than our recording of "Love Bells." This 45 record has proved to be one of the most important events of our collective history as a singing group. It began in the early sixties, and it involved a good friend of mine, Wayne Bramble, who also turned out to be the same guy who first introduced me to the Bobolinks back in 1957.

Wayne and I had run around together for several years before he introduced me to the Bobolinks, and he had always shown a great interest in early rock-and-roll music. Both of us had even sung together in an amateur vocal group in 1956. He also fancied himself as a businessman and always talked about wanting to start a business. He wasn't sure what kind of business he wanted to start, only that he wanted to become a businessman. After a period of time, he decided that he wanted to be in the music business, which seemed like a natural step for him because he was so attuned to the current music scene, and he felt that he knew what the kids wanted to hear.

After talking about it for several weeks, he asked me to go into business with him and start a record company. I had serious doubts for two reasons: First, I had no money, and second, I had absolutely no business background, so I said no. Wayne was undeterred and said that he would do it himself. I asked him where he would get the money to set up this business, and he told me that he had saved some money and thought he could make it work with the amount of money he had on hand. I told him that I would help him in any way I could, and he quickly turned to me and said, "Okay, I love that song "Love Bells," that you guys do, and I want to record it. Will you do it?"

I told Wayne that I would talk to the guys in the group and get back with him. A few days later I spoke with Ronnie Lutz and Jimmy Durst about Wayne's idea, and they showed a lot of interest in the idea. We had no manager at the time and were free to pick and choose our own projects. I arranged a meeting at Wayne's apartment, where we all met and discussed the idea with Wayne and his wife Linda. They had both decided to go into this project as a team, and as a result of that decision, they named their fledgling record company, Way-Lin Records. Many years later, the name of that record company, and more importantly that particular 45 record, would become famous and highly sought after within the record collector's community.

A week after our meeting with Wayne and his wife, Wayne approached a local saxophone player, Ralph McDuffie, who was a well-known member of a local band called the Naturals and asked him to play sax for the recording of "Love Bells." Ralph agreed to the recording session. To this day, I don't know if Ralph was actually paid to do the session, and he doesn't remember either. I don't think it mattered to Ralph as long as he got to play music. From this point on, things get a little murky as far as the details surrounding the recording session of "Love Bells" is concerned. Both Ronnie and I agree that the recording session was held at Capitol Recording Studio in Washington, DC, but we are unsure about a lot of the details of that session. You would think that something so important to our group history would be embedded in our minds, but the passage of time, along with our fading memories once again comes into play.

The details surrounding "Love Bells" even stymie the collector experts. In many of the books about doo-wop history, such as *American Premium Record Guide, 1900–1965* by Les Docks, *The Complete Book of Doo-Wop* by Anthony Gribin and Mathew Schiff, and *Doo-Wop, The Forgotten Third of Rock and Roll* by Gribin and Schiff, the Bobolinks/Memories record of "Love Bells" is listed as having been released in both 1961 and 1962. Even the experts can't agree on when "Love Bells" was first released to the public.

When the recording of "Love Bells" was released, we all felt an immense pride in the quality of our new record. Ralph had done an outstanding job playing sax lead on the record, and we all felt that our vocals were more than up to our own rigid standards. We immediately started to spread the word to our fans in southeast Washington about our new record and how the public could purchase it. Wayne started to network the song among his contacts and the local radio stations. We started to get airplay on the radio stations, and Wayne began to receive a very substantial return of both he and his wife's investment as a result of strong regional sales of "Love Bells." He loved telling me that recording "Love Bells" was one of the best things he ever did, and that I "blew it" by not going into business with him when I had the chance. I think, in retrospect, he might have been right.

Chapter 18

I Lose My Friend

Wayne had always been kind of sickly as a result of being born with the blood disease hemophilia. As a result, Wayne required regular blood transfusions from a well-known Washington, DC hospital. He had been receiving these blood transfusions since he was a child, and he always referred to them as an unpleasant necessity to stay healthy. He never complained about his health, and he was always the optimist where his health was concerned.

Wayne and I remained good friends for the next twenty years. It had been several months since I had last spoken with Wayne when I received a phone call from his wife, telling me that he was seriously ill and in the hospital. I immediately went to the hospital to visit my friend, offer my help, and see for myself how he was doing. I arrived, not quite understanding what was happening, and saw his wife standing outside his room. I asked the usual questions, "Did he have an accident or heart attack?" She would only say, "You'll have to ask him yourself." I was bewildered by both her answer and her attitude, and I quickly left her to go into the room to see my friend.

When I walked into Wayne's room, I was shocked at his appearance. He seemed to have aged overnight into a little old man. I didn't know what to say so I just grabbed his hand and held it. He looked at me and gave me his usual greeting when we would meet, "Pisano, how you doing?" I replied, "I'm doing a little better than you." We both laughed, and he then began to tell me why he was in the hospital. Apparently, as a result of one of his routine blood transfusions, he had been given blood that had not been screened for HIV, and as a result, he now had AIDS and was in the terminal stage of that disease. It got worse! What was even more devastating was that he had passed the virus to his wife. Now I understood why she was acting so strangely.

Wayne then grabbed my hand and asked me to do something that I had never in my life thought I would do. He asked me to deliver his eulogy at his funeral. I had never done anything like that before, and I didn't know the first thing about putting one together. I told him that maybe he should think about getting someone else to deliver it because I probably would mess it up. He insisted that he wanted me to do it. I agreed, although I was pretty messed up at the moment. He was my boyhood friend, and I just couldn't envision him dead. I was physically standing there, holding his hand and talking to him, and the whole idea of his dying didn't seem real to me. I left the hospital numb with grief over the impending loss of my friend, and I felt that the good Lord must have a good reason for taking him.

Wayne died about ten days later, and I honored my promise to my old friend and gave the eulogy at his funeral. At the time, it was probably one of the hardest things I have ever done. Since then, I've had a lot of time to reflect on his passing, and I now know that Wayne had honored our friendship by requesting that I offer his eulogy. To this day, I still think about my old pal and all the good times we shared as young men.

The record "Love Bells" has been intertwined with the Memories history for more than fifty-five years. I can remember receiving many, many calls over the years from record collectors attempting to buy a copy of "Love Bells" from me. They would even find out where we were performing, come to the shows, approach our group members, and harass them in an attempt to buy a copy of the record. Failing that, they would almost always insist that we had copies hidden away, and they would offer to pay whatever we wanted for an original copy. Record collectors are very serious about their hobby. Actually, I should say "their business," because for some, the purchase and sale of collectable records is a big business.

Chapter 19

The "Love Bells" Auction

I would also like to tell you a short story about how a copy of that record was auctioned off. Long after Jim Durst had left the group, Ron Italiano of the United In Group Harmony Association in New Jersey contacted us and asked us to perform at one of their concerts. I checked our calendar, and the date they requested was open, so we accepted the gig. I later found out from Ron (or as we referred to him, Ronnie I) that we would be appearing with Lenny Coco and the Chimes, and the show was for a record collector convention. He also insisted on billing us as the Bobolinks/Memories. We had no problem with that billing and proceeded to go up to New Jersey and do the show. After a pretty good performance, Ronnie called us back to the stage where, unbeknownst to us, they were in the process of auctioning an original copy of "Love Bells" to the audience. We were pretty blown away to see a copy of our record being auctioned and felt proud that people would be willing to pay serious money to own a copy. The bidding began and continued until the record was sold to the highest bidder for the amazing sum of eight hundred dollars. Wow, how cool is that! Ronnie Lutz, to this day, still reminds me that we should have stashed away a few extra copies of "Love Bells" in our attics long ago. Oh well. While still on stage, we had the honor of signing the record sleeve for the successful bidder.

This quest on the part of collectors continues to this day, though not as much as in earlier years. Those of us who performed on that original recording of "Love Bells" feel an immense pride in knowing that what we accomplished as teenagers is still sought after in today's modern day world.

"Love Bells" also played an important part in the Memories being considered for, and later enshrined in The Vocal Group Hall of Fame. It has become so important to us that most of the contracts we receive nowadays from various concert promoters include the requirement that we perform "Love Bells" in our show. I will tell you more about the hall of fame in a later chapter.

Chapter 20

Jimmy Leaves the Group: A New Beginning

I vividly remember this one particular evening because it became a major turning point in our group history. We were rehearsing at Ronnie's house in Forestville, Maryland, and during the rehearsal, Jimmy told us that he was leaving the group. A few months earlier we had all agreed to learn how to play a musical instrument. None of us had done so, and we had all dragged our feet and put off buying the instruments for various reasons. In my particular case, I had been married for just a few months and had a baby on the way, so I didn't have the money at that time to purchase an expensive musical instrument. I also think the money issue applied to most of the guys in the group. Jimmy told us he felt we weren't serious musicians and hadn't kept our promise, so he was quitting the group.

Jimmy wouldn't change his mind, even though we all pleaded with him to reconsider and take some time to think about it. There was no changing his mind. He said good-bye and abruptly left Ronnie's house. A dark gloom seemed to settle over the remainder of us in the room after Jimmy left. I was personally devastated by his quitting, and I didn't think that not buying instruments was a good enough reason for him to leave the group. I thought that it was the end of the Bobolinks. I really believed that we couldn't go on without Jimmy's leadership and drive. He was such a talented and energetic force within the group, and he had also shared with us our dream of making it in show business.

After he left, we all sat there in disbelief and confusion. For the first few minutes, no one said a word. Then suddenly we all had something to say, and a lot of it wasn't nice. We all took shots at Jimmy, most of them not deserved. After we had vented our anger, we decided to talk rationally about the situation and decide if we wanted to stay together as a group. Adversity is a great motivator, and in this case, it got us talking, really talking, about what we wanted to do as a singing group.

I should mention, that almost forty-five years later, Jimmy came back to help out his old pals and sing with us at one of our shows while Boots recuperated from an illness. I remember reminiscing as we started the first song, that the sight of our old friend onstage with us again, brought back vivid memories of a group of young teenage boys, singing their hearts out at teen club dances so many years ago.

After Jimmy left the group, Ronnie and I began the task of trying to lead this group of guys toward what we hoped would be some success in the music business and toward our group's new beginning. For us, it was just one more setback to overcome. We still argued, but became a little more tolerant with one another. That was one very good byproduct of Jimmy's leaving the group.

Chapter 21

Dino

W e decided to restructure the background harmony to make up for the loss of Jimmy's bass/baritone voice and to pick songs for the short term that we already knew. As was usually the case, we argued about almost every song we picked to do, until one or more of us gave in, and we just did the damn songs. After a few months, we realized that we had almost two sets of songs ready to perform in public. We seemed then to get our second wind, and we started to learn lots of new songs.

At this point in time, the group was made up of Boots Dove, Dino Smith, Ronnie Lutz, and me. I should tell you how Dino Smith became the Bobolinks second guitar player. Dick Grimes, our first guitar player, had left the group to start a new job with Safeway Food Stores as a meat butcher, and we were left with no one to play guitar for us. Jimmy Durst knew Dino from his their days at Chamberlin Vocational High School. Jimmy also knew that Dino played guitar, because Dino had recently played with him at a talent show at school.

Jimmy, who was still with our group at that time, brought Dino to one of our practices, and because we really needed a guitar player, we accepted him into the group without a lot of discussion. Dino ended up being a part of the Bobolinks/Memories for many, many years. Dino was probably one of the most quiet and serious members of the group at the time. He didn't possess an outgoing personality, and he usually said very little during rehearsals. Ronnie and I, being prone to playing jokes on one another as well as others, decided to play a joke on Dino one evening after practice.

Chapter 22

Ronnie Shoots Louie

It was just getting dark on a rather hot summer evening when Ronnie approached me and showed me a starter pistol (they don't shoot bullets) that he had just acquired from Larry Lawrenson, a friend of his who was standing nearby. Ronnie took me aside and suggested that we play a joke on Dino. I was all for it. We decided to have Ronnie shoot me with the starter pistol outside the Hi Ho Restaurant after practice.

We decided to set it up with an argument between Ronnie and me over Ronnie's wife. Because Ronnie and I argued all the time anyway (part of Ronnie's resentment still lingered), we thought that Dino wouldn't think our argument anything out the norm. After practice, we all left the Hi Ho together and began to walk up the sidewalk away from the restaurant. Prior to leaving the Hi Ho, I had secretly put some ketchup in the palm of my hand. At this point, Ronnie and I began to argue. Ronnie yelled at me that he was "tired of my crap," and he continued his tirade against me. I began yelling back that he knew where he could shove it, when he pulled the starter pistol out of his pocket, pointed it at me, and said "This ends right now." He pulled the trigger of the gun, and a loud bang rang out. I immediately fell to the ground and began moaning, while at the same time rubbing the ketchup on my face and neck.

Ronnie walked over to where I was lying on the ground. He said, "Maybe next time you'll stay away from my wife." While lying there, I looked over at Dino who was about five feet away from where I was, and he was as white as a sheet. He was looking at me and muttering to himself, when I saw him start inching toward the nearby street. He turned toward Ronnie and said "I want no part of this. I'm leaving." As Dino started to walk away, Buddy, who must have been watching all of this from the doorway of the Hi Ho, walked up to us and asked, "What are you guys up to?" I then stood up, laughing, and Ronnie told Dino, who was still shaking, and Buddy about the joke. I really don't think Dino appreciated the joke, but both Ronnie and I thought it was really funny. We still do.

Chapter 23

The Bass Player

As was usually the case, we ended up being ready to go out and pick up some gigs, but we didn't have any idea where to go to get jobs playing for live audiences. Around this time, we acquired a bass (guitar) man, Jim Morrow. He just happened to be living across the street from my house in Clinton, Maryland. After talking with rest of the group, I invited him over to my house to one of our rehearsals to have him listen to the group and discuss his joining us. The rest is, as they say, history. Jim became a big part of our musical family, and he played with us for many years. He added a lot of personality to our group over the years, and I have several stories about Jim that will illustrate just how much humor he injected into the group with his unusual antics, both onstage and off.

Chapter 24

The Marker Trick

Jim was a very interesting guy, because he could always be counted on to furnish us with lots of laughs with his off-the-wall sense of humor. For example, a few years later after joining the group, we got on him about not wearing black socks with his black group outfit while performing. He became defensive and told us he didn't have any black socks. We all responded, "Tough, Get some." At our next gig, I went up to Jim and demanded to see his socks. He lifted up his pants leg and showed me that he was wearing black socks.

At the time, we were standing on the stage, and the lights were not very bright, so I again asked him to lift up his pant leg, so that I could really see if the socks he had on were actually black. I then noticed that they were not socks at all; Jim had completely colored his ankles black using a marker. The strange thing about this was that they actually looked pretty good. That was Jim Morrow. What an unusual person and jokester he turned out to be.

Another good story about Jim that still makes me laugh was also about his stage outfits. He was notorious for not wearing the right stage outfit at the right time. He would make us very angry when he complained that he couldn't find the outfit he was supposed to wear at our next show. I remember during one of our rehearsals that Jim again complained that he couldn't find the particular outfit that we were supposed to wear at our next show. Ronnie asked him where he had last seen the clothes, and Jim said, "In the trunk of my car." We all then went out to Jim's car to check his trunk for the clothes. At first glance, we didn't see any band clothes in the trunk. One or two seconds later, Ronnie, for whatever reason, lifted up the spare tire, and there were the band clothes lying in the spare tire well, all wrinkled and funky. After a very serious chat with Jim about his responsibility to the rest of the band, we never had a band clothes issue with Jim again.

Chapter 25

An Unruly Crowd

With Jim, you never knew what prank he was going to play on someone or when he was going to do it. For example, on a typical Monday night, we were all onstage at Gus & John's playing our usual dance tunes. A large and boisterous crowd was crowded onto the dance floor, which was not unusual for a Monday night at the club, because we usually filled the place almost every Monday night with hand dancing fans, along with the club's large group of regular customers.

What caught my attention was that in the middle of playing the tune "Aquarius," the dancers on the dance floor suddenly started yelling and laughing. We didn't think anything about it, other than it was the usual craziness associated with our Monday night crowd. A couple of moments later, it happened again, and Ronnie, Boots, and I looked at one another to see if one of us was doing something strange to elicit this kind of response from the crowd. I knew I wasn't doing anything unusual, and both Ron and Boots shook their heads to indicate that they weren't doing anything strange either.

The crowd suddenly erupted with cheering and clapping again. I quickly turned to see if anything was going on behind us onstage, and I spotted Jim quickly pulling his bass guitar down into the normal playing position. By now, all the band members were laughing and pointing at Jim. I caught Jim's eye and mouthed the words "What's going on?" Jim smiled and then turned his bass guitar up so that I could see the back side of his bass.

I couldn't believe what I was seeing! Jim had attached a big picture of a very nude woman in an extremely provocative pose to the back of his guitar, and he had been showing it to the dance floor crowd while we were playing. They seemed to love it! I have to tell you that the picture left nothing to anyone's imagination, and the unruly crowd was yelling for Jim to show it again. On the next break, Jim told me that he had used the centerfold picture from a men's magazine. Even though the degenerates in the crowd seemed to like the picture, I immediately told him to remove it from his bass guitar. Even though Jim had a momentary lapse in judgment, having him in our group was like having Dennis the Menace with us all the time. I have to say that Jim made us laugh a lot, and that's not always a bad thing.

Chapter 26

We Become the Memories

As early as 1960, we began to discuss changing our group name from the Bobolinks to something else. We began to think about changing our group name because we all thought the Bobolinks name was outdated and stale. As a group, we decided in 1962 to adopt the Memories as the new group name, because we felt like most of the oldies songs we were doing at the time were fast becoming "memories," and the new name better reflected the type of music we performed. As it turned out, the new name was a very good choice because the name has withstood the test of time. We have since protected our group name by acquiring the copyright and logo patents for the Memories. It was one of the smartest moves we ever made as a group.

Chapter 27

The Hillary Club

While searching for a new bass player, the Memories were forced to stop accepting gigs for a short period of time. After the Memories acquired Jim Morrow as our bass player, we felt that we were ready to begin performing in public again. Because we now had both a lead guitar and a bass guitar player along with the necessary vocal parts, we were ready to go out and do a good job of entertaining the public. We even purchased a Shure Vocal Master sound system along with enough microphones to enable us to be a self-contained act. When I began to research how we were able to acquire this new sound system for this book, I was unable to pin down exactly how we paid for it. When asked, none of the current or former members of the Bobolinks/Memories could recall how we got the money to purchase the system. Funny thing is we could all remember who went to Chuck Levin's Music Center to pick up our new sound system (Boots and Jim) and how it was transported in Boots's station wagon. It was yet another example of people's inability to recall events from long ago, which frustrates me a little bit.

Around this time, a group of guys that most of us knew from around the southeast area of Washington, DC, approached us with an offer to perform for their organization, the Hillary Club, at a dance they were planning. Because we knew most of the guys in the Hillary Club from a popular local southeast bar called Maxie's, we decided to take the gig.

We figured that it would be a great opportunity to both perform and party with our friends at the same time. We also had the additional incentive of getting paid for our performance. In fact, getting paid was the part that clinched the deal as far as we were concerned.

Chapter 28

Jerry Walmark

To say that we practiced for that gig at the Hillary Club would be an understatement. When the big night came, we were ready to go. Several of us had peeked at the audience from backstage, and we were shocked to see that every available seat was taken. At this time, the Memories had only a lead guitar player and bass player to accompany our vocals. The clock waits for no man, and although we were really nervous, we went onstage and began to sing our first dance set. When we finished the first set, we all went backstage and began to discuss how we felt the set had gone. We were all congratulating ourselves on how well we thought we had sounded, when a guy came into our dressing room and announced, "You guys need a drummer!"

Someone from our group asked, "Yeah, do you know one?"

The guy then said, "Yeah, me." Ronnie told me that he knew this guy from his old neighborhood, and he was a pretty nice guy.

The guy's name was Jerry Walmark, and we began to talk to him about playing drums for the Memories. He told us about some other bands he had formally played with, some we knew, but we needed a drummer so badly that we all pretty much agreed on the spot to accept Jerry into our group. That's how Jerry Walmark became a part of our group and helped to fill a large void in our group structure. Bringing Jerry onboard was a smart move because Jerry was a talented drummer with a great personality and a team player.

Months later, after watching Jerry play the drums numerous times, a few of us began to notice that while playing, he would grimace and then twist his lips in a really funny way. Naturally we nicknamed him Lips, and the name stuck. Jerry was always fun to watch, and over time, we believe he started to secretly enjoy his nickname.

After speaking with Jerry on the night of the show, we were filled with enthusiasm and excitement over getting a drummer for our group, and we went back onstage to finish. Acquiring a drummer was a big step for our group, because it gave us the ability to do much more with our music. We were really pumped up about our newest member, and it showed in the rest of our performance. We finished the show and received a standing ovation from the Hillary Club crowd. That was the first of our many performances for the Hillary Club over the following years. They were our friends as well as a super group of guys.

Chapter 29

Falsely Accused

Speaking of Jerry Walmark, this short story about Jerry involved a member of the Memories being sued and taken to court. What caused this situation to happen began with a gig our group had contracted to perform at the Skyline Inn Hotel in Washington, DC, for an organization called the US Senate Staff Club. The club was having its annual pool cocktail party. Because the Memories had performed for this club several times in the past and enjoyed it, we took the job. On the day of the event, we arrived at the Skyline Inn and began to set up our equipment at poolside.

I spoke with the lady who had hired our group to perform and commented to her that the weather didn't look good for our outdoor performance. I told her that it might rain, and we couldn't safely operate our equipment if that happened. She agreed and told me that she would make arrangements with the hotel staff for us to set up our equipment inside the hotel in the event of rain. Midway through the second set, it began to sprinkle. We immediately turned off all our electrical power sources, and we began to pack up our equipment for the move inside. Breaking down band equipment, transporting it from one place to another, and setting it up again takes time. As it turned out, this interruption of the music to relocate the band from the pool area to another room caused a major problem for us later in the evening.

After setting up our equipment for the second time that evening, we again started to play music. I'm going to brag a bit and mention that we made the transition from poolside to the interior room in record time. Everyone appeared to be having a good time, and the lady who originally hired our group, specifically thanked us for our extra effort in setting up the band equipment for the second time that evening. She also told us how happy she was that we were able to do it so quickly. Everyone—the band, the crowd, and the lady who hired us to do the gig—were all happy, or so we thought at the time.

Later that evening, when the time came to finish up for the night, we played our last song, said goodnight to the audience, and began to pack up our equipment. As was usually the case, I went to find the person who hired us to get paid for our performance. Because of the large crowd, I had a tough time finding her. While I was searching for her, the guys had already loaded our equipment into Jerry's van and had left the hotel. When I finally located her, she blurted out. "You'll have to see Mister so and so for your check." I asked her why we would have to see someone else, when she was the one who had hired us for the gig. She just walked away without saying another word.

I then looked for the person who she directed me to about our money. When I saw him, I approached the gentleman, introduced myself, and asked if he was the person with our money. He introduced himself as the manager of the Skyline Inn Hotel, and said, "I don't have your money. You have to talk to the person who hired you." At that very moment, a big guy came over to us, pointed his finger at me, and said, "You have to talk to me." I could see right away that he was intoxicated, and I told him that I had no business with him. He started to rant and rave about the Memories cheating his club out of thirty minutes of playing time. I honestly tried to explain to him that the thirty minutes he was talking about were the result of us moving from poolside to inside the hotel because of the rain. He became louder and more belligerent, and when I attempted to walk away, he grabbed me by the arm and told me he was a police officer. (I later learned that he was a member of the US Capitol Police Department.)

After he grabbed me, all bets were off as far as I was concerned. I told him that I was not impressed with his being a police officer, that he was drunk, and that I was also a retired police officer, and he was going to get himself into a lot of trouble if he continued to act like a jerk. Again I walked away, only to be followed by this character to the hotel's front steps where he told me he was going to "kick my butt." I had enough! I told the gentleman that if he wanted to "kick my butt," he would have to come down the steps and onto public space where I was standing to do it. All of a sudden, he tumbled down the steps and landed on his backside in the driveway of the hotel. Later I learned that someone had pushed him from behind and that he had sustained a broken leg. How sad!

A few minutes later, I found out that the hotel manager was actually holding our money. It was the same guy whom I had spoken with earlier. He was withholding our money until he received five dollars for a parking sign that Jerry's van had allegedly knocked down when it was leaving the hotel garage with our equipment. In the end, we got our money! Jerry later swore to us he never hit any sign. I really believe that if asked Jerry would even deny ever being at the hotel.

A few months later, the police officer, who had interjected himself into a private transaction that was none of his business, sued me for damages. The case went to court, and he lost the case. By the way, being sued for something you didn't do is kind of scary. Being sued also proved to be very costly to hire the right lawyer to defend myself. To think, this all happened because of a rainy day and Jerry's parking sign fiasco. Anyway, I was very thankful that the truth eventually came out, and that the jury used good old common sense to arrive at the correct verdict. I still get angry though when I think about that whole situation and the stress it put me through. Oh well!

Chapter 30

Aladdin Records and Danny Gatton

I'm going to jump ahead just a little bit, because some of this story about Aladdin Records concerns Jerry Walmark, and I wanted to keep most of what I remembered about him in the same part of this story. It was around late 1970, although I can't remember the exact date, and our group was staying busy performing for numerous organizations and clubs around the greater DC area. Around this time, Jim Durst, Ronnie Lutz, Dino Smith, and I met one evening to write an original group song that we named "Be True My Love." It was just getting dark, and all four of us were sitting in Dino's Coup Deville in front of my apartment just off Mississippi Avenue in southeast Washington. We began to sing various lyrics to the melody we had already decided on. After a short time we narrowed the lyrics down to what we thought we wanted the song to say. It was very hot inside the car because all of the windows were up because it was raining. I remember the windows were completely fogged up, and we had to stop and clean them from time to time. We were all sweating profusely, but having lots of fun.

Being creative isn't always easy, and being in a hot humid car with three other guys certainly proved that point, but we loved what we were doing. We all felt that the song was going to be special, which turned out to be true. We later recorded a demo of the song, loved the way it turned out, and made plans to, at a later date, release the song to the public.

Several months later, a guy named Billy Hancock, who had recently purchased the Aladdin Record label, contacted us and wanted the Memories to sing with his band at a studio recording session and record their song, "American Music." This song was to be one of the first recordings released under his newly purchased Aladdin Record label, and we all felt pretty good about being a part of it. Another part of our deal with Billy was that his band would, if needed, back up our vocals while we recorded "Be True My Love" at the same session. Billy also agreed to release our song on his new Aladdin label. It ended up being a good deal for us, because previous to Billy buying the label, the Aladdin Record label had enjoyed a long and successful reputation in the music business.

We were all pretty excited about recording with Billy because we knew that his group, Danny Gatton and the Fat Boys, would be at the session, and we would be able to spend some time with our old friend Danny Gatton who was scheduled to be there. We found out that the recording session was to be held at Trak Studios in Silver Spring, Maryland, which was very familiar to us from our previous recording sessions there.

The evening of the session arrived, and Jerry Walmark, who was driving his work van, picked us up. Because of a lack of room in the front of the van, we were all piled into the back cargo area , where the first thing I spotted was a couple of cases of beer and some grocery bags. You can probably figure out what was in the bags (liquor) because I did in about two seconds. I realized right then that this recording session might turn out to be one hell of a session. It turned out to be just that!

When we arrived at the studio, everyone was there, and in various stages of getting ready for the recording session. It was like old home week for us because we knew everybody there, but hadn't seen most of them for some time. At that time, the Danny Gatton and the Fat Boys band, consisted of Bill Hancock on bass guitar, Big Dave Elliott on drums, Danny Gatton on lead guitar, and Dick Heintz on keyboards. Ralph McDuffie, our sax man, was also at the session. After wasting a lot of time catching up on the latest news from everyone, we got down to business and began to record the songs that Billy wanted our help with. The session went pretty well, and during the session, most of the musicians and singers paused several times for some liquid refreshment. As a result of those frequent pauses, it started getting pretty wild in the studio. We had a blast!

Chapter 31

Be True My Love: Danny Gatton Plays

We finished the songs that Billy wanted us to do and began to get ready to record our tune, "Be True My Love." We suddenly began to have some problems. Our deal with Billy was that his band would back up our vocals during the recording session if needed. Our problem was that our guitar player, Dino, and our drummer, Tommy DiPietro, were with us in the studio, and they felt that they should play behind our vocals. They had the right to play with us, and Ron and I were placed in the unenviable position of telling Danny Gatton, a national star and personal friend, that our regular guitar player would play for us during the recording of our song.

Danny was cool with the whole thing and said that he would play some back-up leads on the recording if it was okay with everyone. We all agreed that it was a great idea. Big Dave also said he would step aside, and Tommy would play drums for our recording. Everyone seemed happy, or so we thought. Dino still felt a little bit slighted, but then again, almost everyone would feel slighted in the presence of a great guitar player like Danny. Danny added a fantastic lead guitar to our recording of "Be True My Love." For those of you who didn't know Danny, he wasn't just a really nice guy, he was also a genius with a guitar and a pleasure to work with under any circumstances. As a matter of fact, my brother Denny performed with Danny for many years and feels the same way about him that I do. He tragically died a few years ago. But those who knew him, will never forget him or his awesome talent.

Chapter 32

The Master Recording Mix-Up

W hile in the recording studio recording our song for Aladdin Records, it just seemed to be one of those times when everything goes right. The song came out beautifully, and Ralph McDuffie's sax solo had everyone in the studio shaking their heads. It was that good! We thought the song was good to go. We talked to Billy Hancock right after the session, and he told us he was going to mix our song and then contact us to pick up the master. We thought that everything was cool. We unfortunately didn't count on some other folks not keeping their word. That's what we believed at the time.

Many months went by, and we didn't hear from Billy. I tracked him down to find out about the master recording that he promised us. When I finally located him, he was living in Colonial Beach, Virginia. By this time I was so ticked off that when I got him on the phone; I let him have it with both barrels. He immediately denied that he hadn't honored our agreement and said that he had been busy. In fact, he had our master disc right there in his hands. He told me that we could come and pick it up whenever we wanted, which was really good news. Ron and I made plans to go to Colonial Beach and pick up our master. A master recording is simply the final results of your studio work that a sound engineer records on a compact disc. This disc contains the final results that the manufacturer uses to press the CDs that you can then buy in the record stores.

After we picked up our master and listened to it, we found that someone had put a beeping noise throughout the song, which completely ruined it. We also noticed that someone had cut out both Dino and Jim's guitar parts throughout the entire song. As you can guess, both Ron and I were livid. I called Billy, and after several tries, I finally got him on the phone. As I remember it, we kind of told him what we were going to do to him if he didn't make this situation right. Billy, to his credit, said that he didn't know anything about the beeping noise in the song. As far as the bass and lead guitar parts were concerned, he thought that Danny's lead and his own bass part were a much better fit for the song than what our guys recorded.

Billy promised to correct the problem and get back to us. Ron and I decided that the song sounded awesome with both Danny's lead guitar and Billy's bass on the recording. We also knew that for us to go back into the studio to record the song again would be both time-consuming and expensive. Besides, we all loved having Danny playing on one of our recordings. Though it was a win-win for us, we were still left with the major problem of explaining to our guys why their parts were cut from the song, which wasn't easy. Both Dino and Jim had a legitimate gripe, and Ron and I did our best to make them understand that under the circumstances, it was the only choice that we could make at the time. They understood, but they stayed angry about the situation for quite some time.

Billy finally fixed the recording and made arrangements to meet us in Camp Springs, Maryland, with the master disc. After we heard it, Billy was forgiven. The song was beautiful, and Ralph's saxophone solo was a thing of beauty. Furthermore, we will always have a part of Danny with us and can listen to his genius whenever we want.

For the record, that song was later released by MAE Productions as part of an album entitled "Shakin It Up."

Chapter 33

Eddie Leonard's Sandwich Shop: The Jukebox Incident

Hi Ho Records had earlier released the recording of our song, "I Promise," to several commercial record outlets in the Washington area. Our group members had no idea to what extent our record had been circulated in the metropolitan area at the time. So when Ron and I heard our song being played in a commercial establishment for the first time, we were both surprised, and it threw us for a loop.

It was a Saturday night, and we had just finished playing a gig in southeast Washington. While packing our equipment, I casually mentioned to Ron that I was hungry and planned to stop and get a sandwich somewhere. Ron said that he also was hungry and suggested we stop by the Eddie Leonard's Sandwich Shop on Good Hope RoadSE in Anacostia, on the way home.

It was late when we arrived at the sandwich shop, and we were both surprised to see a long line of people in front of us, waiting to place their order for sandwiches. I had decided that I wanted one of Eddie Leonard's tuna sandwiches, and my mouth was watering at the prospect of eating one. Ron and I were standing in line waiting to place our order when we heard our record "I Promise," coming from the jukebox in the corner. We had never heard our song played in public before that time, and both of us stopped and listened with pride to our song. We were both pretty excited, and we wanted to tell the people standing in the line with us that we were the guys singing on that record.

At almost the same moment, the big plate glass window of the sandwich shop exploded, throwing glass all over the shop, forcing both Ron and me to hit the floor to avoid being injured by flying debris. A couple of seconds after we fell to the floor, we heard our record stop playing, followed by a loud screeching sound, as the needle skipped across the record. A police chase had ended with a car crashing through the front of the sandwich shop, turning the jukebox, along with our record, into shambles. We were both pretty bummed out about it, but we were also grateful, because we could have both been severely injured or killed. By the way, no one was injured except the driver, who the police arrested and took to jail. We never did get our sandwiches!

Chapter 34

The Morningside Sportsmen's Club: The Audition

In the spring of 1972, Ronnie and I, along with Jerry Walmark and my brother, Denny, were in the process of opening a record shop on Allentown Way in Camp Springs, Maryland. We called our shop Stax of Wax, and it became not just a retail record store, but also a place for the Memories to both hang out and practice.

Our store had been open for just a few months when a couple of guys came into the store one afternoon and introduced themselves to us as Dick Journey and Mike Mitchell. They said they were members of an organization called the Morningside Sportsmen's Club. They had heard about our group and were interested in hiring us for their upcoming dance. We were very interested because we were always actively looking for the opportunity to perform.

Dick Journey said they wanted to audition us before making up their minds about hiring us. We agreed and set up the audition for our next practice session. At this time, some of our practice sessions were being held at my house in the Crestview subdivision in Prince George's County, Maryland. The location was convenient for most of our group members and also near enough for both members of The Sportsmen's Club to come and audition us.

When the evening of the audition arrived, we were all kind of nervous. We had not performed in public for a while. During that time, we had also added a couple of new musicians to the group. About seven o'clock the doorbell chimed and I invited them to join us in my recreation room downstairs. I introduced them to all the guys in our group and then asked them what songs they wanted to hear.

I had previously given Mike Mitchell a list of songs we were currently doing, so they had a list from which to choose. They asked us to do a couple of songs from the list, and we began to perform the songs they requested. After we finished the songs, they got up as if to leave, and I asked them if they had liked what they heard. Both Dick and Mike said at almost the exact same time, "We loved it! We want you guys to do our dance; Mike will contact Lou about the contract." After they left, I realized that we hadn't even discussed what we would charge them to perform at their dance. At that moment, we really didn't care. We were happy to be singing again and that's all we wanted to do.

We began to practice hard for the Sportsmen's Club gig. On the night of the gig, we were as prepared as we could be and eagerly awaited the start of our performance. The hall was packed with club members, their wives, and guests. Before the show, we were all concerned that the audience might not get up and dance to our music. We also knew that we had to sing four sets to finish the night's performance, and if no one danced, it could be a long and demoralizing night for us. Well, we began to sing, and they danced. Did they ever dance! That crowd danced to every song all night long and actually demanded two encore numbers from us. We were happy to oblige! After that performance, we performed for the Sportsmen's Club many times over the ensuing years.

Chapter 35

The Skyliners' Incident

One of those functions at the Sportsmen's Club turned out to be controversial for the Memories. It involved another vocal group who, at the time, had a top ten recording on the Billboard charts. The group was Jimmy Beaumont and the Skyliners, and the group had been booked to perform at a big dinner dance for the Sportsmen's Club on October 4, 1980, at Sarto Hall. This group was famous for its number one hit, "Since I Don't Have You," which was extremely popular at the time.

Sportsmen's Club member Mike Mitchell contacted us in early September and asked us to perform the opening act for the Skyliners at the club's dinner dance. We, of course, jumped at the chance to open for such a high profile group. We all were very excited to be sharing a stage with one of our group's favorite recording artists.

The trouble started the evening of the big show. We arrived at Sarto Hall and proceeded to go to the designated dressing room for the performers. When we arrived at the door to the dressing room, a gentleman standing in front of the door stopped us and said, "No one is admitted inside but the performers." We told the guy that we were performing that evening, and we needed to get into the dressing room. He again told us that we couldn't go in and that the dressing room was only for the Skyliners. He put his hands on both Ron and I to sort of guide us away from the doorway, and unfortunately, he made a bad decision. I don't think he knew that you don't put your hands on a southeast boy because they always push back.

Ron and I both pushed back and succeeded in knocking him through the dressing room door. At that moment, Boots grabbed us both and told us it wasn't worth the hassle. We left the scene and went to a nearby bathroom to change into our stage outfits. In retrospect, I'm glad that Boots kept his head during this situation because it could have gotten really ugly! An unwritten rule in show business in regards to other performers is that when you're on a show with other recording artists, you always show them the courtesy of not performing any of their hit songs. That was about to change. The Memories knew all the Skyliners hits, and we had performed them many times at different gigs. We had all agreed prior to the show not to do any of the Skyliners hits on the night we worked the show with them. But after being shown such disrespect by the Skyliners, we decided we were going to be petty and do both of their current hit records, "Since I Don't' Have You" and "Pennies from Heaven."

The hall was standing room only. We were ready to go, especially after being disrespected earlier by the Skyliners, and we knew we were going to have a super performance. When we went onstage, the room erupted in applause. We were overwhelmed by our reception and immediately started our performance. After the first number, I looked out into the audience and spotted Jimmy Beaumont, sitting right in the front row center seats. I was still ticked off at him and his group for the way we had been treated. I was also very full of myself as I introduced our next song. I misled the audience and told them that we were going to do a couple of the Skyliners hit songs to "honor" them, which wasn't our intention at all. We wanted to show them that we were not just some pickup band they could look down their noses at. We were all very angry at the time and maybe just over reacted.

We began to perform "Pennies from Heaven" with Denny singing lead, and I immediately followed that by singing the Skyliners blockbuster hit, "Since I Don't Have You." I put everything I had into the songs, and before we even finished the song, the audience was on its feet yelling and applauding. I looked out at the audience and immediately saw that Jimmy Beaumont was also on his feet, applauding. The applause lasted several minutes, and we loved every moment of it. Later in the evening, Jimmy Beaumont approached us and apologized for the dressing room incident. He turned out to be a classy guy, and the Memories have since worked many shows with the Skyliners. Several years later, the people connected with the Vocal Group Hall of Fame told me that Jimmy Beaumont's Skyliners had been one of the groups who recommended the Memories be enshrined in the hall of fame. I write more about the hall of fame later in this book.

Chapter 36

Denny Martin and the Ice Cream Machine

I have referred to Denny several times in this book. Denny is my younger brother. He is also a talented singer in his own right. He was a member of the Memories for more than eight years and was responsible for writing our first stage show and helping us implement it into our performances. Some of the best things about Denny, other than his talent, were his energy and zeal for getting things done and his pressure on the rest of us to learn new material. He also could sing the types of songs that didn't vocally fit either Ronnie or me. By doing so, he could give the public a different sound, which was very important to our group. He was with us all during the seventies when we played at Gus & John's club. He was also able to enjoy the Memories wild and crazy ride through the disco era. Another important aspect of Denny's personality was he would always find food for the band wherever we played our gigs. That was a great asset to our group because of our passion for food.

He, like the rest of us, loved to eat, and he always scouted around to see what food was available, if any, before we began to perform. Once, while we were playing at a hotel located just off the Baltimore Washington Parkway, midway between Washington, DC, and Baltimore, Maryland, we had just finished setting up the band equipment, when Denny peeked out from behind a stage curtain and quietly beckoned for me to follow him. Curious, I did. We walked down a long hallway, and about halfway down the hall, he stopped in front of a soft serve ice cream machine.

I asked him if it worked, and he turned the handle and some soft ice cream started to drip out. That's all we needed to start searching the other backstage rooms for any bowl or cup to hold the ice cream. We didn't care about spoons, but soon found some in a small room adjacent to the ice cream machine.

Denny continued searching and found bowls, and we began to serve ourselves. After enjoying our first bowl, we felt a little guilty and decided to let the other guys in on our find. We first looked around to make sure the coast was clear, then went and told the guys, and it turned into a stampede! It took about thirty minutes of serious eating before we consumed every bit of ice cream the machine held. That machine held a lot of soft serve ice cream, but we met the challenge. Several years later, Denny left our group to form his own band called the Avenue Grand Band. He has enjoyed a lot of success with his band, and he still records and performs with the band to this day. The Memories occasionally supply the vocals for his recording sessions.

Chapter 37

Tommy D'Pietro

As the Memories began to grow, we also realized that our current drummer, Jerry Walmark, wouldn't be with us for the long run. We focused our attention on finding another drummer to take his place. At this particular time, Jim Morrow, who was our original bass player, told us that he knew a drummer who lived in his old neighborhood that might be interested in playing drums for us.

This news was good, but it also presented a problem because Jerry had never given us any definite date for leaving the group. We approached Jerry and told him what we were thinking in terms of bringing a new drummer into the group whenever he was ready to leave. Jerry had been under pressure from his wife for some time to quit the group, and even though we believed he didn't want to leave, he was thinking about it. To Jerry's credit, he agreed that he was thinking about leaving the group, but not right away. He said it would probably be a good idea to bring the new drummer in early, so he could start learning our music before he decided to leave. We all agreed that the new guy could play percussion instruments while serving a sort of apprenticeship program.

It was late 1972 or early 1973, when Jim Morrow first brought Tommy D'Pietro to Ronnie's house to meet the group. Back then, we also practiced behind Ronnie's house in Forestville, Maryland, in a converted garage that was sort of a Memories clubhouse .On the day when Jim first walked in with Tommy D'Pietro, Ronnie, Jerry, Boots, and my brother, Bobby, and I, were just sitting around talking about nothing in particular. Jim introduced Tommy to everyone, and we proceeded to get ready for Tommy's first practice. About that time, Bobby, who had a notoriously quick temper, said something to Tommy, who must have said something smart in reply. Suddenly all we saw was Bobby, lunging across the couch toward Tommy with murder in his eyes. Tommy leaped out of Bobby's way to avoid being hit, and we all converged on Bobby to try and stop him from continuing his attack on Tommy. Finally, cooler heads prevailed, and after talking about it with Bobby, we found out what had caused the confrontation.

Tommy simply misunderstood the way things were done in our neighborhood compared to where he grew up. Tommy was only sixteen years old at the time, and he probably wasn't used to being around a bunch of older guys from southeast Washington. He probably interacted with Bobby the way he was used to doing with kids his own age. What he didn't know at the time was that guys from southeast DC demanded mutual respect and some deference from folks who were not from the southeast area. It was a southeast thing! They worked out everything, and they never had any further problems between them. Years later, after he retired, Tommy told me that the Bobby incident was simply an "oil and water" situation.

When Jerry retired from the Memories, Tommy took over the drummer position and became an immediate hit with the girls. He was young, cute, and Italian. By the way, most of the clubs we worked in at the time, including Michelle's, Brass Lantern, Gus & John's, Joe Theismann's, and so on, had they known Tommy's age at the time, would not have allowed him to play in their clubs because he was too young to work in an establishment that served alcoholic beverages. Tommy went on to perform with us for more than thirty years. You could honestly say that he grew up with us.

I had occasion to speak with Tommy about his recollection of the early years he spent with the Memories. What he told me during the interview both surprised and flattered me. Tommy told me that when he first met the group, he had been "intimidated' by the overall group talent. He said that he had been so "overwhelmed" with the group during the early years that he had given up most of his high school activities to perform with us. What he said next really made me feel good. He said, "You guys became like father figures to me." That was not our original intent, but we're sure glad it worked out that way. Tommy was very special to us, and he ended up being not just a drummer, but a dear friend for life to Ronnie, Boots, and me. While thinking about the time Tommy spent with us, I can't help but realize that Tommy, more or less, grew up with the guys in the band. Thank God we didn't totally ruin him.

Tommy met his wife Cathy while he was with the Memories, and he has become a devoted family man with three lovely children. He now divides his time between his family, work, and his church activities. The Memories still miss him to this day, and when he has the occasion to come see us in concert, we take a lot of pleasure in introducing him to our audiences. He paid his dues and he deserves it!

Chapter 38

The Gus & John's Audition

The record shop proved to be more than just a retail record store and rehearsal hall for the Memories. Our store was also responsible for our group getting numerous gigs during the time we owned the shop. For example, after we had been open awhile, we put our heads together to find a way to boost record sales at our shop. We decided that because we had a band/vocal group, along with all the necessary equipment we needed on hand, we should set up the equipment in front of the shop one Saturday afternoon and have our group perform live in hopes of drawing customers to our store. We also knew that my brother Bobby had a friend who was one of the owners of Prince George's County, Maryland's hottest night clubs, Gus & John's, and we thought he could probably get him to come hear us play. After hearing us, we hoped he would hire us to play at his club.

Our plan couldn't have turned out any better. The weather was beautiful, and the people started showing up at our store right after we began to play. We played music for about two hours, and then, bitterly disappointed, decided that Bobby wasn't going to make it. We called it quits and began to pack up the equipment. Right before we got any of the equipment packed, my brother showed up with one of the owners of Gus & John's, Gus Petrides. He seemed like a real nice guy and told me that he had heard a lot about our group and would like to hear us play. My big brother had come through for us big time!

We quickly got things hooked back up and began to play. Gus was like a kid in a candy store, and he seemed to really enjoy the group. After our third song, he stopped us said, "Come on over to the club and we can get you started. You're hired." What we didn't know at the time was the audition for Gus Petrides would change the course of our group history and open many doors that we could never have imagined for the Memories.

That was the beginning of the longest running job in the Memories history. We worked at Gus & John's, and later at Michelle's after the club name changed, for more than twelve years. The years we worked at both clubs turned out to be some of the most exciting, fun-filled happening years of the Memories history! For most of the early years, we played only Monday nights, but that changed when we were enticed with more money to play Sunday nights. I write more about both of those night clubs later.

Chapter 39

The Middle Years: Gus & John's

Y ou will recall, that earlier, I told the story about how Gus Petrides, one of the owners of Gus & John's night club, stopped by our record shop one Saturday afternoon, and auditioned our group while we were playing music in the parking lot in front of our record store. That was the actual beginning of what turned out to be, more than decade of success at Gus & John's, and Michelle's night club.

The time the Memories spent working at Gus & John's during the seventies and eighties was magical. As performers, we were living the dream. We had a steady gig, making good money at the time, and we had hoards of loyal fans that followed us and supported our group. What was not to like!

The club was located on Old Branch Avenue in Temple Hills, Maryland. Although the area was not the best for operating a nightclub, it was not the worst either. It never seemed to have any trouble in attracting lots of customers from all over the metropolitan area. The club even had its share of nationally known sports celebrities (Frank Howard from the Washington Senators, Sonny Jurgenson from the Washington Redskins, and more than one gentleman from Washington's hockey team,) who made their way to the club from time to time.

I don't know exactly what made Gus & John's so special, but I have a pretty good idea. Gus & John's was unique because of its location, its entertainment, its great bartenders, and its reputation for catering to the area's building and trades contractors. Those four ingredients, mixed together for more than a decade, made Gus & John's the place to see and be seen in the metro area.

The club's location was almost perfect for those living and working in the Washington area. It was just a couple of miles from the beltway and only a couple of blocks from a major north-south highway (Route 5), which ran into the District of Columbia and was only five minutes from Andrews Air Force Base.

Gus & John's was so business-friendly that many of the area's young building trades contractors who worked in the surrounding areas conducted a lot of their business from booths located in the front bar of the club. One local contractor even had a dedicated business phone line installed in one of the booths where he spent a lot of time, both conducting business and enjoying the club ambiance. Later in the evening hours, you could usually find a serious high stakes card game upstairs.

The third part of what made Gus & John's so special was the level of entertainment at the club. Most nightclubs have pretty decent entertainment most of the time. Gus & John's had great bands all the time. They were known for providing the best dance bands in the whole metropolitan area, and it showed in the number of people who packed the place night after night. At one point, the club had two bands playing at the same time. One band would play behind the front bar and another would play in the back bar area, separated by a thin wall.

Chapter 40

Ralph McDuffie

When I first walked into Gus & John's, I saw a band playing behind the front bar. I realized that I knew this group, the Naturals, from the southeast area, and I had performed with them on a couple of occasions in the past. The irony was that the group's saxophone player, Ralph McDuffie, was the original sax player for our very successful record, "Love Bells," in 1962. Ralph immediately began to bring me up to speed with information we needed to know about working at Gus & John's. Ralph ended up playing with the Memories off and on for more than thirty-five years until retiring from our group in 2004 and moving to Florida with his wife Jane.

Ralph is the kind of saxophone player who comes along once in a lifetime as far as I am concerned. He intuitively knows what notes need to be played and when to play them. We never had to tell Ralph what we wanted him to play, because he just knew what was needed in the song to make it better. If there was a better fifties-style sax man within five hundred miles of DC, we never met them. People liked Ralph's soft-spoken and unassuming personality. He was never one to put on airs, and everyone who knew him always felt comfortable in his presence. Ralph spoke so softly that, from time to time, some of the guys would tease him about it and ask him to stop mumbling. He never took offense. He truly is a gentleman and a real professional in the way he leads his life. He is also the best saxophone player I have ever had the honor to work with. All of the Memories are proud to call Ralph our friend.

Chapter 41

Monday Nights at Gus & John's

The Memories started our new gig performing at Gus & John's on Monday nights. Gus told us that the reason he wanted us to play Monday nights was that it was the slowest night of the week for his bar business, and he wanted to see if we could bring enough people into the club to make Monday nights profitable. We began to perform at the club, figuring the worst that could happen to us was to get fired for not bringing in enough business. Working at Gus & John's was our first club gig as a group, and we didn't know what to expect from either the bar patrons or the management, so we decided to perform like always—full speed ahead. We started having fun!

The guys in the band loved it! Lots of girls were always around, and the booze, if you drank it, was usually free to the group members. In addition, we were playing in the hottest nightclub in the DC area. What was not to like about it. What we didn't know at the time was just how much work went into staying current with the public's fickle music tastes. We were also not aware of how important it was to look out for one other while performing onstage and also while on our breaks. We were soon to learn all that and much more. A popular nightclub has a vibrancy and feel all its own, and we quickly learned to anticipate the mood of the crowds as well as their propensity for violence when too much alcohol was consumed.

Chapter 42

Success Pays Dividends

During our long tenure at Gus & John's, we were wildly successful in building up both the club's Sunday and Monday night business. We, as a group, would often talk about how much money the owners were making, and we felt that we should share in the wealth, too! We decided to approach the owners with a request for a raise. We had previously heard from some of the other groups who played at Gus & John's, that it was not a good idea to ask for a raise at that particular time. We decided to go ahead with our request anyway. After a Monday night show, when all the customers had left the club, we packed up our equipment, and Ronnie and I went to the owner's office.

When we walked into the owner's office, Gus Petridis, one of the club's owners and the one who had originally hired us, stood up from his desk and said, "I'm glad you came to see me, because I was going to send for you guys." He added, "You guys have done an outstanding job, and I want to give you guys a raise." In all the years we worked for Gus, he always beat us to the punch where raises were concerned. Both Ronnie and I often asked ourselves, how both Gus and John, always seemed to know just when to give our group a raise in pay. In all the years we worked at Gus & John's, never again did we have to ask for a raise. Both Gus and his partner John were wonderful to work for. Almost thirty years later, I found out that both Gus and John were alumni of Eastern High School, which was also where I attended. I wish I had known this sooner; I might have been able to use it when the bosses would occasionally get ticked off at us.

Chapter 43

Gus and John Show Off

Gus and John were not only good businessmen, but they also were role models for the guys in our band, who for a lot of reasons looked up to them. First, they owned one of the area's hottest nightclubs. Second, they were both making lots of money. Third, they often had beautiful young women hanging around the two of them most of the time, which young guys like us really envied. Another plus for them was their flamboyance when interacting with the club's customers. They always seemed to know just what to say, when to say it, and the exact time to buy a round of drinks for the regulars at the bar. It was quite a performance, and it worked really well for them.

One incident that really made me envious and showed some of the flamboyance I spoke of occurred one summer afternoon when my brother Bobby and I stopped by the club to see a friend of his. As we got out of our car, the club door opened, and both Gus and John walked out with two gorgeous young blondes. They walked over to two brand-new, identical Lincolns, got into them, and drove out of the club's parking lot with barely a good-bye wave to us. Wow! I was really jealous of the whole scene. I wanted that to be me. Who wouldn't be enticed with lots of money, beautiful girls, and luxury cars? After they drove away, I turned to my brother and said, "I think the Memories need a raise." My brother Bobby looked at me and, in his wisdom (he was my older brother), said, "Better be satisfied with what you guys are getting and don't start getting greedy." Bobby was always one to get right to the heart of the matter, and he was right! You just can't beat common sense.

Chapter 44

Sunday Nights: Double Our Fun, Double Our Pay

After being very successful in building the Monday night business to where the club was making good money, both Gus and John decided we should also play every Sunday night too! They told us that Sunday nights needed a boost in business, especially during the Washington Redskins football season. The club sponsored a bus trip every Sunday to RFK Stadium for all the Redskins home games, and after the game, the bus returned to Gus & John's to unload its rowdy and mostly inebriated crowd.

Their reasoning was simple: Keep the bus crowd in the club for a while, sell lots of booze, and make some money. Playing on Sunday nights sounded like fun to us, but it put us right back behind the eight ball again. We had to grow the crowd for Sunday nights, just like we did for Monday nights at the club. This request also put additional pressure on some of the guys in our group who had day jobs to consider. The addition of Sunday night to our performing schedule meant that the guys with day jobs faced two consecutive nights of getting home well after three o'clock in the morning, which left them just enough time to get cleaned up and ready to leave for their day job. I've already mentioned how both Gus and John were sharp businessmen, and again they proved it with another substantial raise for the Memories.

We all agreed that the money we were now getting paid made the loss of sleep worthwhile. Gus later told me that we were the highest paid band at their club. That information became food for our group's healthy ego.

We started playing both Sunday and Monday nights, and we continued to be very successful in building up the crowd for both of those so called "off nights." The interesting thing about both of those nights was that the crowds were, for the most part, entirely different. Pinpointing exactly how they were different is difficult, other than Sundays crowd was slightly older and more affluent than the Monday night crowd. The Sunday night group also was already primed with plenty of alcohol from the Redskins game and the bus ride by the time they arrived back at the club. Another interesting aspect of our Sunday night crowd was we began to notice that some of them were also starting to come to the club on Monday nights and vice versa. Performing on those two nights was probably the most fun our group ever had up to that point in time.

While interviewing people for this book, I spoke with John Linthicum, one of the original owners of Gus & John's. He told me that both he and Gus had been extremely happy with the Memories during the years we worked for them at their club because our group, with our successful Sunday and Monday nights performances, gave them, in effect, two Fridays and Saturdays of profits for the week. He said, "What club owners wouldn't have been happy with those kinds of results." In 1975, John sold his interest in the club and invested in a successful real estate company on Capitol Hill in Washington, DC. He later married and moved to Florida. Ronnie and I bumped into John in 2011 while doing a show in Myrtle Beach, South Carolina., and we enjoyed sharing some memories. No pun intended.

Chapter 45

Gus & John's Unpredictable Customers: Thirsty

A funny incident that occurred during our stint at Gus & John's involved a club regular I nicknamed, Thirsty. Thirsty was a scruffy, sneaky-looking guy who was a club regular, though he could never be called a customer of the club, because he almost never spent any money for drinks while in the club. While performing onstage and over a period of several weeks, I began to notice him walking around the club with what appeared to be a drink glass in his hand, which was not unusual. What I saw him do was unusual.

Every time our band played a very popular dance song, a lot of the crowd would go to the dance floor to dance. While they were dancing, Thirsty would wander around to the various tables, take a quick look around, and pick up other people's drinks and pour the contents into his glass. Our boy never had to pay for his drinks. What amazed me about him was he was never caught or punched out by the people whose drinks he was stealing. . He was also never carried out of the club on a stretcher despite all the different types of alcohol he drank. The human body is amazing!

Chapter 46

Attacked from Behind

Another not-so-funny incident involved yours truly getting jumped by a group of guys who had come to the club one night to celebrate their friend's bachelor party. By the time they arrived at the club, they had already enjoyed their party a bit too much, and most of them were drunk. Toward the end of one of our band breaks, I had gone to the front bar to get a diet soda. On the way to the bar, someone goosed me from behind, and I hollered over my shoulder to whoever it was that "I hoped you enjoyed that." I was used to the club regulars joking around, and the guys in the band traded insults and bantering with the customers all the time. I thought that this was one of those times. Unbeknownst to me, this particular event took place when one of the guys from the bachelor party thought that someone from the band was messing around with his off-again, on-again girlfriend who worked at the club as a bartender. Being a band member made me a prime target.

A moment after I was goosed, a blow to the back of my head knocked me to the floor. I suddenly was face down on the floor, with several guys on top of me, trying to beat the hell out of me. I covered my head and tried to protect myself, when I realized that none of the guys on top of me were actually hitting me. So many guys were on top of me that they were hitting each other in their attempts to get to me. Out of the corner of my eye I saw a hand outstretched to me, so I grabbed it and was pulled from under the mob. My benefactor turned out to be Bobby Hesterberg, a big guy who frequented Gus & John's, and who was also a part-time bouncer at various clubs in the area. After Bobby pulled me from under the pile of angry drunks, I watched as they continued to beat on each other for several more minutes. In a strange way, it really was fun to watch. As far as I was concerned, no harm occurred, so no foul. Bobby later told me that he felt it was not a fair fight, and I needed a little help. After the fight ended and cooler heads had prevailed, some of my assailants apologized, and like most bar fights, all was forgiven. Several years later, Bobby was shot and killed during a botched robbery at his place of business. He was one of the good guys.

Chapter 47

The Snake

Something most people don't know about a band playing in a club is that they not only sing and play instruments, but they also get to see a lot of interesting things that happen in the club from their vantage point onstage. For instance, we could usually see which guy was trying to move in on another guy's girl when the guy she came with left her to go to the bar and get them drinks. Sometimes it worked, and sometimes it didn't. This particular night it didn't work. The snake moving in on the other guy's girl was well known to all the band members for this kind of move. This time though, unbeknownst to the snake, the waitress had intercepted the girl's date before he made it to the bar and had taken their drink order so he was able to get back more quickly to their table. When her date arrived back at the table, the snake was trying to put his hand where it wasn't supposed to be and was having considerable success.

When her date saw what was happening, he went after the guy, and they both began to circle the table while throwing their drink glasses and screaming threats at one another. These two clowns gave an award-winning performance. They were both so drunk, and the band members knew they didn't really want to fight each other, so we did what we thought was the right thing, we began encouraging them from the bandstand. This funny scene went on until the girl in question got up and left the club. She was drunk too! The guys continued on for an additional few minutes until the bouncers got tired of the show and threw them both out of the club. The next time we saw these same two guys together, they were sitting at the front bar, telling war stories like best friends. Go figure.

Chapter 48

The Girl at the Urinal

During our tenure at the club, we became accustomed to seeing a lot of bizarre actions from our customers and fans. One incident involved yours truly that caused a lot of personal embarrassment. We were playing our usual Monday night gig at the club, and the dance floor was crowded with lots of people who were in a real party mood. The Memories had just completed our first set of the evening, and I had to go to the bathroom to relieve myself. That in itself is not particularly unusual, but what happened next was. I was standing in front of the urinal, when the door opened and a beautiful young girl came in and hopped up onto the sink right next to where I was standing.

I frankly didn't know what to say. I was so embarrassed that I stopped what I was doing and attempted to put myself together and leave the bathroom. The young lady would have none of that, and she actually put her hand out to stop me from leaving the bathroom. I quickly realized that she was intoxicated and attempted to reason with her. She grabbed my shirt. While I was attempting to pry her hands off various parts of my anatomy, she slipped into the sink. The water somehow came on and began to wet her bottom, which was firmly wedged in the sink at the time. That was my signal to make my escape as fast as I could, and I did. It wasn't because she was unattractive; she was beautiful, but that scene was just not for me. When we started the next set, she was on the dance floor, dancing her totally wet bottom off. We all laughed so hard that we messed up the song and had to start it again. She never caught on to what we were laughing about.

Author's first singing group, 1956: L-R W.Bramble,
J.Lee, R. Jasper, J.Smith, L. Martin

The Memories, 1972: Top L-R L. Martin, R. Lutz, R.Dove, Sr., Bottom: D.Smith, T.D'Pietro, J. Morrow

The Memories, 1970: L-R J.Morrow, R. Lutz, L.
Martin, T.D'Pietro, J. Walmark, R. Dove Sr., D. Smith

A young Tommy D'Pietro on drums, 1973

The Memories, Late seventies: Top: L-R, L. Martin, R.Dove Sr., D. Martin,B. Taylor, Bottom: T.D'Pietro, R. Lutz, R. Bautista,J.Morrow

Admission Ticket for Sportsmen Club dance
with The Skyliners and The memories

The Memories, 1978: L-R, R.McDuffie,R.Dove, Sr., J.Morrow,L.
Martin,B.Taylor, D.Martin,T.D'Pietro,D.Smith,R.Lutz

The Memories 25th Anniversary Party at Gus&John's club with Lou Martin receiving the Memories governors citation from Md. state Delegate Joe Vallario, and Md. state senator Thomas (Mike) Miller Jr.

Mid seventies outside photo of The Memories after a performance.

The Memories: Top: L-R R.McDuffie, D.Martin, D.Smith, Bottom:
L-R, R.Dove Sr., L.Martin, T.D'Pietro, J.Morow, R.Lutz, B.Taylor

Glenn's first concert performance as a singer at the Long Island
Coliseum: L-R: R. Dove Sr., R.Lutz, L. Martin, G. Bortz

Our Vocal group Hall of Fame visit: L-R:
L. Martin, D. Martin, R.Lutz

The Memories Vocal Group Hall
of Fame Museum display case.

Lou Martin standing in front of The memories Hall of Fame Museum display case.

Singing in the stars dressing room at the Vocal Group Hall of
Fame with: L-R, L.Martin, Jack Hunt (Johnny Angel& the
Halos,) T. D'Pietro, G.Bortz, R. Lutz, R. Dove Sr.

Hall of Fame VIP's: L-R, L. Martin The Memories, with Tim Hauser, Manhatten Transfer, Al Jardine, The Beach Boys, Tony Buttala, The Lettermen, Warren Suttles, The Ravens.

Memories in the Vocal Group Hall of Fame performance hall:
L-R, R.Dove Sr., T.D'Pietro,G.Bortz,L.Martin, R. Lutz.

The Memories performing at the 2000 Vocal Group hall of Fame induction concert.

Lou Martin singing with Mary Wilson and her two replacement
backup singers at the Vocal Group Hall of Fame Ohio concert.

Memories reunion party: L-R, Top: L. Martin, R.Dove Sr., Bottom: Original member, Jim Durst, T.D'Pietro,R.Lutz, V.D'Orazio.

Memories group photo: L-R, Top: G. Bortz, Rob Dove Jr., Charlie Helmick, V. D'Orazio, Bottom: L-R, L. Martin, R.Lutz, N.Arena.

L-R, Lou Martin with Pookie Hudson of The Spaniels,
and Ron Lutz at the Wama awards show.

The Memories perform: L-R, Ron Lutz, Lou Martin, Neal Arena.

The Memories celebrate their 53rd anniversary: Top; L-R: C. Helmick, R.Dove Jr., R.Williamson, M.Scheer, Bottom: L. Martin, R.Lutz, G. Bortz.

The Memories, 2011. Top: L-R, C.Helmick, R.Dove Jr., R.Williamson, M.Scheer,Bottom: L. Martin, N. Arena, R. Lutz.

On capitol hill with L-R: Diz Russell, The Orioles, Charlie Thomas, The Drifters, Lou Martin, The Memories, Bill Pinkney, The Drifters, helping F.A.M.E. lobby for laws to protect against the unlawful use of a singing group's identity by other persons.

The Memories first group photo with newest addition to
their group. June Flynn (center of photo.)

Chapter 49

The Microphone Incident

It must have been a full moon that night, because a little later that same evening, another very pretty and slightly inebriated young girl came up to the stage and beckoned for me to bend down so that she could talk to me. Club patrons often came up to the stage while we were performing to request songs, so I thought nothing about her coming up. What never ceased to amaze me and the other singers was that club patrons never seemed to understand that a singer couldn't hold an intelligent conversation with them and continue to sing a song at the same time.

In the interest of public relations, I bent down anyways to listen to the request she wanted to make. She leaned in real close, and because it was very loud right in front of the bandstand, she had to shout to be heard. At that time, she was shouting directly into my ear, and I was holding my microphone in front of my mouth while still trying to sing the song. When the song ended, she was still shouting in my ear, and what she said to me came out loud and very clear over the PA system. She was telling me and sharing in great detail with the other club patrons at the same time exactly what she wanted to do to me after I finished work for the night. The crowd erupted in applause and catcalls. It was just another crazy night at the club, filled with unpredictable crowd behavior. It wasn't always fun!

Chapter 50

Boots Has Surgery

An important aspect of performing on a regular basis in a nightclub is the health of the group members. The public usually takes for granted that when they show up at a club, a band will be waiting to entertain them. That's fair and is usually the case where club bands are concerned. However, performing groups consist of human beings, and occasionally, they get sick or incur a short-term disability. For the most part, over the years, our group had been very lucky in this regard. That was about to change.

The first instance occurred when our original baritone Boots fell from the stadium roof and seriously injured his spine while working at his day job at RFK Stadium. This injury required him to have major surgery to repair his spine and extensive post-operation therapy to get back to normal. This presented a serious problem for our group because Boots was the foundation for our harmony. His absence threw us completely off balance from a vocal standpoint. Ron and I put our heads together and decided that some of the other group members would need to step up and sing a harmony part, which turned out to be the beginning for a couple of our band members (who did not normally sing) to begin to sing with the existing vocals. In the short term, it strengthened our group vocals, but it required a lot of work from the established vocalists to coach the new singers. In the long term, it gave us the viability of being able to call on the extra vocals when the tunes needed them.

The Memories held Boots in such high regard that as soon as we thought he was able; we attempted to entice him back to the Gus & John's stage to perform with us. We needed Boots so badly that we were finally able to talk him into coming back to perform with us a bit earlier than he had anticipated. He had previously mentioned to us that the doctors wouldn't let him stand for any extended periods of time, so we arranged to have a chair onstage for Boots to sit in while singing. This was a first for the club because no other band in the club's short history had ever had a band member perform while sitting in a chair onstage. The plan worked great, and we had our pal back with us. It was great to hear that harmony once again.

Chapter 51

Boots Disappears

Speaking of Boots, I have to tell the story about his one and only invisible performance while he was with the Memories. Boots's injury required major surgery and a long post-op recovery time. In the later part of his recovery, the group enticed (more like begged) him to begin performing with the group before he was fully recovered. As luck would have it, his performing didn't cause him to have a setback in his recovery, and things were once again looking good for our group unity.

Boots had been back performing with our group for a few weeks, and we were scheduled to perform for the Fraternal Order of Police annual dinner dance at the prestigious Shoreham Hotel in Washington, DC. This event was a very big affair that most of the law enforcement personnel in the greater metropolitan area along with most of the local politicians attended. The Memories had always looked forward to this event because of the venue and the size of the crowd. Both my brother Denny and I were members of the Fraternal Order of Police. As a member of the board of directors of the District of Columbia's Fraternal Order of Police lodge #001, I would personally know a large number of people attending this event.

The big day came, and we arrived early to supervise the setup of our band equipment. Everyone was in a good mood, and the ballroom began to fill with the guests. While standing around onstage, Boots happened to glance out into the audience and spotted his boss from the DC Stadium Authority, talking with the DC Mayor Marion Berry. Boots panicked!

He called Ronnie and me together behind the stage curtains and told us that he couldn't go onstage and perform. Both Ronnie and I wanted to know why he couldn't perform because we were just minutes away from the start of our show.

Boots told us that he was still on sick leave. If his boss saw him onstage performing, he could lose his job and his medical benefits. We understood his problem, but it left us with a big problem of our own and only a few minutes to solve it before our show began. Ronnie and I racked our brains, trying to find a solution to our dilemma. We were just about at our wit's end, when someone said, "Let's hide Boots!" At the moment, that statement didn't make any sense to me, and I remember rudely saying, "Shut the hell up, and give us a minute to think." We were under a lot of stress. Not only were we the main attraction at the event, but thousands of people also were in the audience, waiting to see us perform, and among them were a lot of our friends from our lodge.

We were so keyed up at that moment that we almost decided to just go out and do our show without Boots singing with us. It suddenly dawned on us that we might have a solution to the problem. I really don't know who suggested it, but whoever it was, deserved a medal for such a great idea. We knew that we had a couple of very long microphone chords in our gang box, and one of our group members suggested that we replace Boots's shorter microphone chord with our longest microphone chord and then run the chord behind the stage curtain where Boots could hide. He could still sing his part without letting his boss see him.

What a great idea! Our stage crew set it up, and the show began without Boots being out front onstage with us. Some of the people up close to the stage knew something was amiss, and a couple of the guys from our lodge even yelled out to us about our missing man. We didn't miss a beat, and we performed our first show without even so much as a hiccup. Being able to hear Boots sing through the monitors and not having him physically standing next to us onstage did seem kind of weird.

After our first show, we all went back behind the curtains to congratulate Boots on doing a great job even though he wasn't there! Boots laughed and said, "I love being invisible." I left the stage area to go out into the audience and visit with some of my friends from my lodge, and Boots chose to remain back stage and out of sight. When we later returned to the dressing room to get ready for our second show, Boots was very excited to report that his boss had left the hotel, and he could now go onstage with us.

The rest of the show went great, although some of our rowdy friends seated in front of the stage, razzed us about our invisible man's dramatic reappearance. We still talk about that "Invisible Man Show" to this day.

Chapter 52

The Toad Runs Over Ronnie

This funny incident occurred to one of our group members, Ronnie, during the winter, when he stopped by Gus & John's one afternoon to have a drink with some friends.

Ronnie, being the friendly guy that he is, was having so much fun that he might have stayed at the club a bit too long. After a final drink, he realized that he had consumed too much alcohol and decided to leave the club and go home. Ronnie later told me that he was "drunk as a skunk." When he attempted to put the key in his car door lock, he passed out, fell to the ground, and rolled under the car parked next to his vehicle. Two other factors proved to be very important to the story. First, while Ronnie was inside the club having a great time, it began to snow rather heavily. The second factor was that one of the guys Ronnie had been drinking with that evening was a fellow named Donnie Kauffman. Donnie had the unique distinction of having the nickname Toad.

He honestly came by the nickname, because he somewhat resembled a toad because he was short and round, and he had a face only a mother could love. Toad was a really fun guy to be around, had personality plus, and could really consume large quantities of alcohol. I mean large quantities of alcohol! Almost everyone who knew Toad either loved him or hated him, and there seemed to be no middle ground where Toad was concerned. While Ronnie was lying under the car outside in the snow, Toad decided that he had had enough to drink and he left the club.

As Toad made his unsteady way to his vehicle with the snow coming down, he got inside and started the car. Toad didn't know that Ronnie had rolled under his car and passed out. Toad, although drunk, started the car and attempted to back out of his parking space. He stepped on the gas, and his car started to move backward until it hit an obstacle. He pulled forward and again put the car in reverse. He then gave it more gas and again attempted to back over what he thought was a pile of snow under his car.

Meanwhile, Ronnie woke up and saw a car muffler just above his head. He also felt an intense pain in his chest where the car wheel had tried to run over him. He quickly realized that the car over him was backing up again and was going to hit him. Ronnie began to yell as loud as he could. The car stopped, and Ronnie saw a pair of feet standing in the snow by his head.

Toad's head peered under the car at Ronnie as Ronnie desperately tried to pull himself from under the car. Toad then staggered back into the club and announced to everyone that he had run over Ronnie with his car. Everyone in the inebriated crowd got into the act, giving lots of booze-induced advice and providing varying degrees of assistance as they followed Toad to the parking lot. They eventually drove Ronnie to the hospital, and guess who was driving? Toad! Not only was Toad drunk, he didn't possess a valid license to drive. While driving to the hospital, Toad turned to Rose, Ronnie's significant other at the time and told her that if the police pulled them over, for her to jump over him and get behind the wheel. Guess what? She was pretty much blitzed too!

Chapter 53

The Hospital

After they arrived at the hospital, the staff proceeded to remove the shredded jacket and shirt that Ronnie was wearing to prepare him for X-rays. Unfortunately for the X-ray technician, every time she stood Ron up to be X-rayed, he toppled over. He was still drunk. The hospital staff also had difficulty getting any coherent information from any of the people who came with Ron to the hospital.

Eventually the staff squared away everything, and Ron was treated for several broken ribs and deep lacerations to his chest. As a result of the accident, our group gave Ronnie, who was considerably heavier at the time, the nickname of The Whale. Most of the guys in the band had already started to call him The Whale, because he was carrying so much weight around. Wasn't that sweet! We could be a rotten bunch at times, but we loved Ronnie.

To show what a true professional he was, Ronnie, who had been run over by the Toad just a couple of days earlier, went onstage with our group to perform. Although still tightly bandaged around his chest, he sang his buns off. However, during the performance, I just couldn't let this chance go by to comment on his unfortunate accident. I stopped the show and told everyone all about how the "The Toad ran over the Whale." My story was a hit. Everyone talked about it for months, and some people still remember it to this day. Ronnie was a good sport about it, and I honestly think that Ronnie has even begun to enjoy the tale.

Chapter 56

Side Jobs

The Memories received side jobs as a result of our performing at Gus& John's and Michelle's for more than a decade. Our group became so popular during that period of time that we were fortunate enough to stay very busy performing at lots of other venues in the tri-state area. Not only did we perform at Gus & John's on Sunday and Monday nights, we also performed Friday and Saturday nights at many other outside events.

I'll tell you about the group's crazy time trying to fit all our bookings into our already heavily booked schedule a little later. Looking back on it, I think our need of money overwhelmed our common sense.

Chapter 57

The Weddings

We stayed busy performing at bar mitzvahs, bat mitzvahs, anniversary parties, birthday parties, corporate events, political rallies (even though we didn't always agree with our employer's politics), various social clubs, volunteer fire department events, fraternal order of police functions, weddings, radio stations, and numerous fraternal groups, such as the Elks, the Moose, the American Legion, and the VFW.

As for the weddings, the Memories estimated that we have played for more than five hundred weddings during our history together. We have also joked that we have played for every organization that had antlers. We performed at so many weddings that we developed a rating system for them. We rated the wedding on loose criteria, such as how late we would start our performance because of wedding photos being taken with the wedding party back at the church or, because of the interference of the so-called wedding planners. Next on our rating scale was the number of cute girls in the wedding party. The final, most important rating criteria, was the food offered at the reception.

Chapter 58

Our First Big Mistake

The food at wedding receptions was important to us because the band was usually invited to eat during our breaks. The truth is that most of us were always hungry, and some of the guys in our group could really put away the food. Even when we were not invited to eat at the reception, some of us would line up and get served anyway. If the food was considered good by the majority of our group, the rating for that particular wedding increased. But when the food was lousy, the overall rating we gave to that particular wedding reception took a nosedive. It really didn't matter to us though, because we ate everything.

I remember one particular wedding reception, which involved a gaffe I made. Although it wasn't my fault, it still bothers me to this day. We had a format we used when we played weddings. We talked to the bride and groom beforehand and asked numerous questions, such as wedding music they would like to have played and when they wanted the band to make any announcements or introductions, such as the first dance, the cake cutting, the removal and throwing of the garter, and the throwing of the bouquet. All of these things were pro forma for our group during a wedding.

At this particular wedding reception, the problem began when I inquired about the pairings for the first dance. Usually the first dance starts with the bride and groom dancing first as man and wife. Then the father of the bride dances with the new bride and the mother of the groom dances with the new groom. The band then invites the wedding party to the dance floor to join the newlyweds and parents for a group dance. Next, the band invites the general public to join everyone on the dance floor. This lineup occasionally varied. Here is where it got dicey. I spoke with the bride just before the wedding and inquired if she had any changes in the program. She replied no. Just before we announced the bridal party, I again asked if there were any changes she wanted me to know about. Again, she said no.

When the first dance began, I announced the new bride and groom's first dance. They took to the dance floor and began to dance. No problem so far. The next step was to ask the bride's father and the groom's mother to join them. I did. A moment of silence suddenly fell in the hall, followed by a loud crying and shouts of anger. Unbeknownst to me, one week prior to the wedding, the bride's father had passed away. The bride and groom decided to go forward with the wedding, and for whatever reason, they neglected to tell me about this development when I asked them if there were any changes I needed to know about. To say our band was embarrassed would be an understatement.

After the dust settled, the bride was kind enough to take the microphone and tell the audience that it wasn't our fault. The wedding went on, and everyone seemed to enjoy both the free liquor and our music. Not everything goes smoothly when dealing with the public. When looking back at all the weddings at which we performed, I am proud to point to that particular wedding as our only snafu. We played for more than five hundred weddings in our group history. We also consumed a lot of wedding reception food.

Chapter 59

The Wedding Planner

In almost all the weddings where we performed that had a wedding planner running the show, things never went smoothly. One major incident comes to mind and still makes me laugh. This incident involved the fancy wedding of a well-known lawyer from Prince George's County, Maryland.

On the day of the wedding, we arrived at the reception in an extravagant hotel and began to set up the band equipment. A woman almost immediately approached us and began to issue instructions as to how we were to perform for the wedding reception. Anyone who knows our group can say that we are an independent-minded group of musicians who don't take kindly to people telling us how to do our jobs. It wasn't the best way to start a gig, and I asked the woman, "Who are you?" She informed me that she was the wedding planner and was in charge of the reception. While she was telling us how to do our jobs, things were happening all around her to which she seemed unaware.

I later learned from a staff member that she had already alienated most of the serving staff with her snobbish, overbearing attitude and petty demands. The staff decided to do things its own way. Whenever she turned her back, the staff did exactly that. What occurred next was classic.

While she was conducting her tirade against the serving staff and giving us instructions on how to perform, between two and three hundred guests had arrived at the ballroom and began seating themselves. The ceremony at the church had taken a long time, it was late in the afternoon, and the guests were hungry.

The servers immediately began to place all the finger foods, fruit, shrimp, cheeses, and other snacks on the serving tables. Even though the bride and groom hadn't arrived yet, it took just one guest to approach the serving table and start to fill his small plate, when a hoard of people descended on the food.

I never have understood how this "professional" wedding planner could not have known that in addition to the wedding party being more than an hour late arriving at the reception, it was also late in the afternoon and the guests were very hungry and looking for some food to nibble on.

The wedding planner started yelling at the guests that they could have the food in a few minutes and to please wait. She was too late. In a matter of minutes, both of the long tables had been swept clean of every bit of food. The wedding planner sensed that the wedding reception was getting out of control and flipped out. She then approached the bandstand and ordered us to start playing music. We declined. She then angrily demanded that we start playing immediately or else. We again declined. I had decided early on that she might become a problem, so I had a copy of the contract for this gig in my pocket. I pulled out the contract and showed her that our starting time began when the bride and groom arrived at the hotel ballroom. I also took the opportunity to remind her that we worked directly for the bride's family and not her.

By this time, the staff was fully involved with their continuing revolt against the wedding planner and had begun to serve the dinner early. This must have been the last straw for this particular wedding planner because no one saw her for the rest of the evening. Later, during one of our breaks, I approached the bride's father and relayed to him what had happened prior to his arriving at the hotel ballroom. He surprised me by saying, "I kind of thought that was the situation; she was a bit too pushy for my tastes." He also said, "The guests liked the food, and they were hungry. I was too, and as long as the food wasn't wasted, I'm satisfied." If he was happy, we were happy too!

Chapter 60

Too Much Success

While we still played at Gus & John's, during the holiday season, we often were so busy, playing outside gigs that we found ourselves working almost seven nights a week. Playing that much almost caused our group to break up. We may have been making lots of money at the time, but all the musicians were exhausted, and the vocalists had become hoarse and were in danger of losing their voices. We were all so cranky and tired, that while performing, some of us had resorted to yelling derogatory comments at one another while onstage. Boots once kicked a tambourine across the stage that almost hit Rudy in the head. Kicking an instrument was a major no-no. Another time, Boots sneaked out into the audience and threw some ice cubes toward the stage in an attempt to make us laugh. One ice cube hit me in the face and totally messed up my ability to sing the song. We all laughed, and I thought it was kind of funny at the time and knew Boots meant me no harm.

Realizing what was going on, we all got together and decided that no matter how good the money was, our group unity was more important. We decided to immediately cut our bookings in half, and it turned out to be one of the best group decisions we ever made.

Chapter 61

An Unusual Situation: The Great Escape

During the late seventies, we received a call from the owner of a brand new nightclub called, Rogers I, asking if we would be available to perform for his grand opening party. The club was located in a small town located on the shore of Chesapeake Bay, Maryland, called North Beach. Nobody in our group knew anything about this new club, but we decided to take the gig anyway. We all felt that because we rarely performed in that particular area anyway, why not do the gig and maybe get some additional work from other commercial establishments in that area of southern Maryland.

On the night of the gig, one of the crew met us at the door and told us we weren't going to be happy with the band setup inside the club. He said the club was very small, and the band setup was in the back corner of the room. I've always hated playing in small venues where we are forced to squeeze our equipment into a small, tight space.

We proceeded into the club to check it out. When our crew member told us that it was small, he wasn't kidding. It was a disaster in the making for us, because we needed room to move around when performing, and this setup left us with no room for our vocalists to maneuver. After venting my anger, which didn't help the situation at all, we finally figured out how to configure the stage setup to give us additional room.

The club started to fill early, and it was full by ShowTime. To the delight of some of the band members, the crowd was comprised of about seventy percent females. When I say crowd, I mean the club could only hold about 120 people. The crowd seemed to be having a great time, and the band members were enjoying the audience response to our music. A large group of young women sat right in front of the stage and were particularly taken with certain band members. During the course of the evening, they decided they would be going home with the band members when we finished our show.

None of us had suggested to any of these young ladies that they go with us after the show. It was just another wild and crazy fan night for the Memories. After the show, the club slowly emptied, and the crew proceeded to pack up our equipment. Around this time one of the group members said a group of girls were waiting around the corner, and they had just told him that they were going home with us when we left the club. I wanted no part of this, and the other fellows felt the same way. We had all worked hard, and we wanted nothing more than to unpack, store our equipment, and go home to get some sleep.

We decided that we needed a plan of escape from these young women, which is exactly what we did. We agreed that the two trucks with the equipment would use different routes when they left the club area. We also decided to not talk with the girls when we left the club so as not to encourage them.

Our plan didn't work. When the crew told us the trucks were packed and ready to leave, we ran for the trucks and attempted to make a quick exit before the girls could follow. They outsmarted us. They had two cars loaded with girls, already waiting when we ran for our trucks. We took off, and they proceeded to chase us. We tried going in circles and making numerous turns in the hope of dissuading them, but to no avail. One of our trucks was an open bed pickup truck that we used for the smaller equipment, and while attempting a fast turn, some pieces of our equipment fell off the truck, which required our guys to stop the truck, get out, and go back to pick up the equipment.

Here we were, trying to flee from a bunch of pretty young girls at three o'clock in the morning. We were all tired and had worked hard, trying to entertain our audience. All we wanted to do was to go home and get some sleep. The truck that I was riding in finally ditched the car following us by hiding behind a gas station in the Wayson's Corner area in southern Maryland. I still laugh, thinking about us hiding from a car full of cute girls behind a gas station in the early hours of the morning. Those were the days!

We later found out from our guys in the other truck that after some good-natured kidding, the girls finally realized that to continue the chase was futile and left after giving the guys their phone numbers. Being a member of a band will expose you to a lot of temptation, and you have to be strong enough to use good common sense when these types of situations arise. During the many years we've been together, not all of us were successful. Maybe adversity comes with the territory!

Chapter 62

The Memories Twenty-Fifth Anniversary Party

During the time we played at Gus & John's, Washington, DC's hottest oldies radio station WMOD hired us to be its official band. As a result, we performed at numerous cool venues and had our music played on the radio. We played at the Back Alley Lounge in Bladensburg, Maryland, for WMOD for a long time. Life was good for the Memories, and we were later honored with a group twenty-fifth anniversary party at Gus & John's. On the night of the celebration, almost all the metro newspapers had reporters at the club to cover the story. Where reporters are, politicians aren't far away. In this case, the politicians were all over the club, shaking the hands of the band members and the hundreds of customers who crowded the club. So many people showed up that the bouncers had to restrict access to the club because of fire regulations. Half of the Maryland State Legislature appeared to be there, and the Memories were presented a proclamation from both the Maryland House of Delegates and the Maryland State Senate. We were feeling special.

The band members were suitably impressed at the time, because we had never heard of this happening for any other musical group in our area. We also had the added pleasure and prestige of having the Maryland State Senate President Mike Miller Jr. (a big oldies fan) personally present the State Senate proclamation to us all. Most of the press photographers who were there captured the moment, which enabled us to have a printed memory of the occasion. At the time, we all felt that it couldn't get any better. Again, we were wrong. It got better!

Not long after receiving the proclamation from the Maryland State Senate, another public agency honored us. Prince George's County Sheriff James Aluisi honored each of our group members with a proclamation that named us honorary Prince George's County deputy sheriffs. The honor was kind of interesting, because two members of our group were retired members of the Metropolitan Police Department of Washington, DC. Despite that, we were all deeply touched by the honor, and over the ensuing years we became very good friends with Sheriff Aluisi. He is truly one of the good guys.

Another honor we are very proud of has been our ability to assist others in need. Most people only know the Memories by our reputation or by watching our performances at different venues around the country. We have been blessed to be able to help others through the use of our collective talent. We have had the honor of performing for national charities, such as the American Cancer Society, the Muscular Dystrophy Association, the American Heart Association, and others. We have also assisted numerous other national groups with their fundraisers for the critically ill. We consider this a blessing and a privilege.

Chapter 63

Gus & John's Closes Its Doors

The one constant in life is change. I realized that our string of luck couldn't continue forever and decided early on to just enjoy the ride. In 1975, I heard through the grapevine that John had sold his interest in the club to Gus and had left to go into the real estate business in DC. The news made me a little sad because those two guys had been very successful together, and our group also had enjoyed their success. I began to worry that things at the club would not be the same with John gone. That wasn't the case at all. Things continued on as before, and the Memories continued our wild ride with success.

In early 1979, our wild ride at Gus & John's came to an end. Gus decided to close the club, and we went to work performing at other venues. We didn't have any problem getting a lot of work, because we were well known in the metro area as the "real deal" and the only original white doo-wop group from the era of early rock-and-roll who was still performing. Lots of club owners were clamoring to get us into their clubs to perform. Our group was not so naive as to believe these club owners wanted us solely for our doo-wop history. We knew they really wanted us because of our fans and the dollars they would bring to a club when following us.

After leaving Gus & John's, we continued to play at the Back Alley in Bladensburg, Maryland, as the official band for oldies radio station WMOD. WMOD later became WMZQ and changed its format from oldies to country music. We had a lot of fun playing at the Back Alley, and celebrities, like our boyhood friend, Danny Gatton, would stop by to listen to our group and occasionally sit and play with us. Danny was a very talented guitar player and a nationally recognized star who was still a down-to-earth guy. Some of our group members had known Danny many years prior to his phenomenal success when he was living on Elmira Street in southwest Washington, DC. As a matter of fact, my family lived just a few doors down from Danny's house on Elmira Street. The Memories were fortunate to have Danny play on two of our successful albums, "Shaking It Up" and "Lost and Found" on the MAE label. We all treasure our memories of Danny, a truly nice guy.

Chapter 64

Michelle's

In the next few months, we played at a succession of club venues, such as Gentlemen's III, Villa D'Este, (later changed to the New Yorker), and Michelle's. While playing at the Villa D'Este, the new owner of Gus & John's, now called Michelle's, asked us to come back and play for them. At the time, we personally didn't know the new owners or anything about them. We later found out that both of the new club owners were former metropolitan police officers Barry Haslup and Jose Cruz. Although both my brother Denny and I were retired from the Metropolitan Police Department, we had never worked on the job with either one of the new owners.

Barry contacted Denny, who was handling the group bookings at the time. He asked if we would be interested in leaving the Villa D'Este to come play at Michelle's. Denny negotiated a raise with Barry that would give each man an additional ten dollars per night. We were already primed to leave the Villa D'Este because of our problems with the owner over the way he treated us about getting paid. After we finished our nightly performance and went to get paid, he always insisted that we wait until he had cashed out all his cash drawers. We didn't care about his cash drawer situation. We only cared that we had done our job for the night and wanted to be paid without waiting until three o'clock in the morning. Several of our group members had day jobs they had to get ready for, and waiting around to get paid was robbing them of much needed sleep. We had several nasty arguments with the owner about this situation, only to have him do the same thing over and over again. We were ready for a change when Barry called us.

We made the move to Michelle's and had only been there a short time when Denny came to the rest of the group and told us that Joe Theismann of Washington Redskins fame, who also was part owner of a nearby club bearing his name, had personally called him and asked if the Memories would be interested in playing at his nightclub. He offered more money, and we voted as a group to make the move over to Theismann's club. The move proved to be short lived. After playing there for about a month, Barry contacted us and asked us to come back to Michelle's with a nice raise in pay. Being the greedy types, we all agreed to go back to our old club. We never regretted that decision.

Barry later told me that he had received threatening calls from our old boss at the Villa after we had left to go to Michelle's. Our old boss at Villa told Barry that he was going to suffer bodily harm for taking us away from Villa. Barry said that he took the threats very seriously, and for several weeks he carefully checked his house and car before going anywhere or doing anything to make sure no explosives were planted. These threats all turned out to be just a lot of hot air from the Villa owner, who fancied himself as some sort of Mafia Don.

Because we shared a history of being former police officers with the new club owners of Michelle's, we quickly became friends during the years that we played for them. Michelle's was a lot like the old Gus & John's in the sense that almost everyone that went there to have a good time usually succeeded. Part of the success of both of the clubs (Gus & John's and Michelle's) was the direct result of a lot of people who grew up in southeast Washington, coming to the club and supporting it. It became a sort of meeting place for the southeast folks to get together, dance, and catch up with their old friends.

Chapter 65

The Memories Say Good-Bye to Michelle's

In 1982, everything started to unravel at Michelle's when Barry told us that he was going to sell his interest in the club to Jose Cruz, his partner. When Barry sold and gave up his hands-on management style of the club, we experienced a parade of different managers who brought a variety of management styles to the club. None of them worked, and the Memories saw the handwriting on the wall and began to plan on when we would leave Michelle's. Not long after Barry left the club, the Memories sadly bid a sad farewell to what had become a very big part of our lives.

To say that leaving what amounted to be our musical home was not traumatic for us would be an understatement. We had grown up a lot in that club, and it meant a lot to us all. For me, every time I went to work at Gus & John's or Michelle's, it was like going into my own personal club. As a matter of fact, we were so involved with the club that Ronnie actually built the stage that all the bands performed on at Gus &John's and later Michelle's. It was a decade-long party and not easy to just walk away from, but we had to.

In the years after both Gus & John's and Michelle's closed, and before we achieved some success on a national scale, the Memories remained in demand by both club owners and numerous private venues. We even played more weddings! Our group personnel later dramatically changed, and our group received some much-deserved recognition in the music industry.

Chapter 66

Glenn Bortz and the Big Show

In 1988, the Memories were performing at a charity event in Clinton, Maryland, at the American Legion for a young cancer victim. Rudy Bautista, who was once again playing lead guitar for the Memories, approached me and asked if he should talk to a bass player that he knew from another band called Landslide, about joining our group. This other group coincidentally was also playing at that same charity event. We had recently lost our original bass man, Jim Morrow, and we were actively looking for his replacement.

Ron and I discussed it for a moment, and then we gave Rudy the go-ahead to speak with the bass player. Rudy came back after a few minutes and said that the bass player, Glenn Bortz, would like to audition for our group, and Rudy had set it up for the following week at Bill's house. When the next practice rolled around, Glenn showed up and was introduced to everyone. We began to discuss the audition songs we wanted him to do. Some of us were a little worried about him because he was from Virginia, and we kind of thought that most people from Virginia were a little weird. (Just kidding!) At the time, we all thought Maryland was the center of the universe. (We now think differently!) We later discovered that Glenn had lived in Maryland for quite a while, which made him all right. Glenn played a few songs with us, and we were convinced! He was hired, and we have never been sorry!

Several years later to show how much of a team player Glenn became, he started singing vocals as well as playing bass guitar with the Memories. In March 2000, Dino, our lead guitarist, and Bill, our keyboard player at the time, declined to do an upcoming show at the Long Island Coliseum. This show was huge, with more than twenty-five of the best vocal groups of the 1950s and 1960s appearing in concert. (I list some of the performers here.) We had been invited to appear, and it personally and professionally meant a great deal to us to perform at the show.

The Skyliners, Del Vikings, Tokens, Chantells,
The Platters, Bobby Rydel, The Cadillacs,
The Drifters, Cleftones, Danny & the Jrs,
Maxine Brown, The Memories, The Harptones,
Frankie Ford, The Marcels,
The Planotones, Five Discs, Mel Carter

The Memories had been performing and rehearsing for what seemed like a very long time. When our friends, The Cleftones and Diz Russell of the Orioles, asked us to appear with them on one of the biggest doo-wop shows in several years, we were blown away. The show was to take place in two week's time at the Long Island Coliseum in New York.

I was very excited about this opportunity and immediately spoke with the guys in our group about the show. As I was telling them about our invitation to perform at the show, I noticed an apparent lack of enthusiasm on the part of both Dino and Bill toward our participation in this big concert. When I pushed the issue, they both gave vague excuses for not wanting to do the show. Bill cited family issues, and Dino simply said he wouldn't go. Both Ronnie and I were furious with both of them, and we decided right then that the Memories would perform at the show anyway. We also decided that both Bill and Dino would no longer be a part of the Memories future.

Chapter 67

Glenn Steps Up

G lenn immediately volunteered to step in and sing with us at the show, even though he was our bass player and not a singer. For him to do this meant many, many hours of practice time to learn the vocal parts that he would now be singing. He also would have to learn all those parts in just a couple of weeks. Glenn jumped in one hundred percent and gave it his all. On the day of the concert, after a long bus ride with several other acts appearing on the same show, including the Orioles, the Rainbows, and the Jewels, we finally made it to the Coliseum. Glenn will always remember that bus ride, because of the broken toilet on the bus that he was seated right across from the entire way to the gig. The whole bus smelled like raw sewage. When we finally made it to our dressing room, a guy walked in right behind us and asked if we were the Bobolinks. We said yes, and he introduced himself as one of the Five Discs, a really talented group of guys who were also appearing on the show that day. He said that his manager wanted him to check us out, because his manager had heard that all the Bobolinks were dead. We assured him that we were still alive. He asked us to not go anywhere and he would be right back. I think they thought we were lying about being the original Bobolinks.

We continued to get ready for our show, and about five minutes later, he returned with all of the Five Discs and their manager. For whatever reason, they seemed amazed that any of us were still alive. Boots, Ronnie, and I assured them that we were the real thing and still very much alive.

They considered us one of the pioneers of the early rock-and-roll vocal groups, which really pleased us. After a few minutes of conversation, they timidly asked us for our autographs, and if we had any personal memorabilia we could give them. We signed autographs for them and gave them what group stuff we had on hand, which seemed to please them. Performers almost never ask other performers for their autograph. It's just not usually done. We all felt honored and extremely flattered by this attention, especially from such a great group of singers.

Chapter 68

The House Band

Because of the size of the show, the crowd, and all the big name groups we were performing with that night, we were extremely nervous. We waited to perform and worried that the house band might not be able to play behind us. We had been listening to the other groups perform, and we didn't think the house band was doing a very good job playing for most of the groups who went onstage before we did. A house band is the group of musicians that the promoters hire who play for the many different acts that appear on a particular show. The same band plays throughout the whole show. The various acts that are contracted to appear on that particular show are required to send their musical charts to the promoter weeks in advance of the show date. In theory, doing so allows the house band to rehearse all the music well before the actual show date. We decided to make sure that the band knew our music before we went onstage.

When the first intermission came around, we went to visit the band members in their dressing room and asked them to rehearse privately with us. Some of them said they were tired, but we persisted and they finally gave in and said they would. Thank God we did insist! They didn't have a clue as to what we wanted them to play. They probably hadn't even looked at the musical charts we had sent to the promoter weeks earlier. Fortunately for our group, I had brought a cassette recording with me of the songs we were going to perform onstage, and after we got them to listen to it, they began to pay attention to what we wanted them to do. After a few minutes with them, we left their dressing room feeling a little bit better about the band. I still had some reservations about this so-called house band and said a little prayer that they would at least look at our sheet music before we started our performance.

We went on, performed, and received a standing ovation from the thousands of doo-wop fans in the audience despite the band not doing a very good job of backing us. I was totally surprised with the standing ovation and just reveled in the applause. My prayer was answered. Glenn came through for us with flying colors! We never even missed Dino's vocals that day.

Our participation in that show became a turning point in the Memories career. From that point on, we began to receive the recognition and respect from our peers within the music industry that we had been seeking. National promoters began calling, and we started to appear all over the country with most of the national music acts from the fifties and sixties. It was a dream come true to be able to refer to many big name performers from the early rock-and-roll era as our friends.

From that point on, Glenn has played an important part in both his singing, as well as playing the bass guitar for our group. How does he do both things at the same time? I've always wondered about that. He has now been with the Memories for almost twenty-five years. He is third on the seniority list with our group, and I consider him to be a very dear friend.

Much later, while talking with Glenn about our group, he told me that he had first heard the Memories play a couple of years earlier at a show for the Fraternal Order of Police at the Shoreham Hotel in Washington, DC. The band he was playing with at the time, Horizon, was going to be the opening act for the Memories at the same event. He told me that he had been very impressed with our group, and later, when asked by Rudy if he was interested in trying out for the Memories, he jumped at the chance.

Glenn also related how he and some of his buddies from his workplace at the US Census Bureau would often go to Gus & John's club on Monday nights to listen to the Memories play and enjoy a few beers. Along with being a super musician, Glenn makes a killer rum cake! My waistline thanks him.

Chapter 69

The Recording Studio

I've written an awful lot about the Bobolinks/Memories history, and I thought that you might enjoy reading about the laborious recording process that most professional musicians go through to bring to the public a product that is both polished and ready for sale.

The first thing that occurs, at least with our group, is the selection of tunes we wish to record. A lot of thought goes into this portion of the decision-making process because the right selection of songs is critical to the commercial success of any new album. In our case, our production team gathered a list of the old rhythm and blues/doo-wop tunes that they thought our fans might enjoy listening to, and then all of us (the production team and our group) got together and made our selections from the final list of songs. We also considered some of our own original songs along with the other tunes selected for recording.

After we finished arguing about the song list, we started to rehearse the songs to be recorded on the new album. This part of the process took quite a bit of time, because both the vocals and the musicians had to learn the material before we even thought about going into the studio to record. Everyone had his own strong opinions about what he thought sounded good, which is a good thing because sometimes our musicians came up with great ideas for some of the songs we would be recording.

During the process, our production team also researched the mechanical and copyright history of the songs chosen for our album, so they can take care of the payments for the rights to record the songs, which can become quite expensive.

Up to this point, this process has taken several months, and we now have a handle on the songs for our new album. The album usually will contain anywhere from ten to twelve songs, and getting all the songs studio ready is one very big job. While the rehearsal process is still ongoing, the production team is busy working on the graphics along with the interior text design for the new album cover. I personally like this portion of the process, because a sharp, visually attractive CD cover helps with album sales.

The production team has already met with the studio representative and scheduled the studio time we'll need to record and mix the songs that will eventually appear on our new album. We have been fortunate over the last ten to fifteen years to be able to work with the same sound engineer who has helped us with our last few albums. The sound engineer, Ron Vinto of Nightsky Studio, has been blessed with incredible hearing, which is essential to that particular vocation. He continually amazes us with his ability to pick out both vocal and musical flaws during the recording process.

I can't say that I always agree with him when he points out that I went flat on a particular song, but I know in my heart that he's right and only wants our best product to come from his studio. All the guys feel the same way about Ron because we've always been proud of the finished product.

What happens in the studio usually follows a predictable pattern. First, the musicians go into the studio to record the music for all the tunes for the new album. This process can take several weeks to several months. To give the musicians some reference point, the vocalists come to the studio and sing scratch vocals.

Scratch vocals means we sing the songs just to give the musicians a vocal reference of how the vocals fit their music format. These scratch vocals are then discarded and never used. The musician portion of recording is both difficult and tiresome for the musicians because it takes so much time to get everything just right. It's not unusual for the musicians to do twenty takes to get one tiny portion of a song to the point that it's acceptable to the engineer and production team. Not surprisingly, the musicians often express a lot of volatile opinions during these long and very tiresome sessions. In the end, not only are these guys professional musicians, they're all good friends, so it always works out.

The vocalists next come into the studio. The vocalists time is even more tedious than the musicians' time in the studio. While in the studio, Ron quickly brings down to earth the vocalists with a resounding crash, when he points out how bad we sound on a particular song. He is also good at picking out the vocalist who is off key by pointing out his or her flaws in the vocals.

One of the worst things about studio work is finding out just how bad you can sound on a particular song. The engineer has the ability to isolate everyone's vocals and often does so during the recording process. The hardest part is being able to take the trash talk from the other guys in the group, when the engineer isolates and then plays back that individual's vocal for all to hear. It makes a vocalist very humble!

This part of the process also takes several weeks to several months to finish. After all the music and vocal tracks are finished, the really critical part of the recording process begins. This part of the album process, called editing and mixing, can take many months to complete.

During the mixing process, every beat of the drums, every hit on a cymbal, and every note played on the keyboard, the guitars, the saxophone, and any additional percussion instruments, is individually checked for tuning, balance, and tone.

Just listening to every beat a drummer makes on his drum kit during just one song can last about twenty minutes. As a result, the mixing process can take a very long time to complete. After the musical portion of the recording, the process moves to the vocal sessions.

While mixing the vocal portion of the recordings, the engineer must listen to every note that every singer sings on every song. He has to listen for tonal quality, timing errors, and vocal blending of the background harmony, and he must also apply the same criteria to the lead vocal parts.

The engineer then puts the music and vocals together, and then reviews the overall sound blend again. What emerges is the same product sold at a retail music outlet.

The process seems so complicated compared to when a group called the Bobolinks recorded for Colt 45 Record Company so many years ago. Back then, the studio engineer bunched all the background singers around just one microphone while the lead singer was a few feet away behind a movable wall with sound insulation stuck to it to deaden the sound. Back then they recorded us on tape, and mistakes took forever to fix because they had to do it by hand with clear tape and razor blades.

Today, when recording, we are all put into different cubicles with our own individual microphones and headsets. Most of the time, we can't even see the other vocalists we are recording with, and all communication between the vocalist and the recording engineer is through the headset. Furthermore, everything in the modern studio is digital, and mistakes, although they still take time, are much easier to fix. I hope this brief overview of the recording process helps give you a better understanding of how much work goes into producing the music that we all listen to and enjoy. It's certainly not easy, but if it was, then anyone could do it!

Chapter 70

The Glory Years

After the Memories performed at the big doo-wop show in Long Island, New York, some of the bigger promoters in the music business finally started noticing us. That's not to say that we weren't noticed in all the years that preceded that show; we were. However that particular show had a large gathering of nationally known performers and promoters who took serious notice of our group. That particular show had more than twenty-five national acts performing that drew thousands of fans to the Long Island Coliseum. After our live performance in front of thousands of doo-wop fans, the Memories received a standing ovation. I honestly felt that we deserved it!

I vividly remember that after we came off stage, Herb Cox of the Cleftones, grabbed me by the arm and told me that we had done one "helluva job." On the way back to our dressing room, we received accolades from many of the other performers who were standing in the hallway, waiting their turn to go onstage. Receiving this recognition was amazing to us, and it meant so much for our peers to notice our work. We had always felt that we had the talent to perform with the big acts and knew that all we needed was that one opportunity to show what we could do. It finally happened. With our new vocal addition (Glenn), we seized the moment.

When we returned home after the big show, we were still on an emotional high. We had held our own and received a standing ovation for our performance. It was the turning point in our history. We had finally made our mark in this business and that good things were going to start happening for us. I have to thank Diz Russell of The Orioles and his wife Millie for getting the promoters of that big event to invite the Memories to perform. The Orioles have, over the years, consistently encouraged and supported our work. In addition, Millie Russell, a promoter in her own right, has on numerous occasions also hired our group to perform along with other acts for oldie shows she has promoted.

We had only been back a couple of weeks after our performance at the big show when we began to receive inquiries from several different promoters about performing for them at various shows around the country. That news was great for our group, but it also raised some very serious problems that our group had to face before we could commit to any new shows. As a result of our previous keyboard player and lead guitar player not performing with us at the Long Island show, we had separated them from our group. That left us with pending gigs, and no keyboard or lead guitar player. What a terrible position to be in. Ronnie and I were both nervous wrecks.

We stalled the promoters as best we could, while frantically looking for both a new keyboard player and a lead guitar player. Finding people in the business that are talented enough, know the music, and fit in our band was quite difficult. This problem, however, turned out to be another blessing in disguise for the Memories.

Chapter 71

Vince (Vinnie) D'orazio: The Basement

The Memories lost Dino as our long-time lead guitar player, and we were looking all over for someone to replace him. Our bass guitar man, Glenn Bortz, mentioned that he knew a lead guitar player named Alan Cloutier. He thought Allen was a pretty good musician, so we invited him to one of our practice sessions to audition. Alan showed up the following week at our practice with another guy and explained to us that he had thought it over and could not commit to the time we required of him to play with us on a regular basis.

He said that he had brought a friend with him, Vince D'Orazio, who also played lead guitar and who wanted to audition for our group. We agreed to it and decided on a song that Vince could play for his audition. We began to sing the song, and Vince began to play along with us. After the song finished, we decided that Vince didn't seem to be an experienced guitar player, but we only needed someone to play chords for us so we could sing. We decided to have Vince join the Memories. From that point on, he became Vinnie to us.

During Vinnie's audition with our group, Ralph McDuffie, our sax player, had not been available, so he did not have the opportunity to meet Vinnie. At our next practice, while getting ready to start rehearsing, Ralph leaned over to Vinnie and asked, "Where have you played?" Vinnie turned to Ralph and said, "In the basement." Because the rehearsal room was a little noisy, Ralph leaned in a little closer to Vinnie and asked,

"Where?" Vinnie again repeated, "In the basement." Ralph seemed to think about it for a moment, and then said to Vinnie, "I've never heard of that place before." Vinnie replied, a little louder so Ralph could hear, "In my basement." Ralph took a moment and then burst out laughing. At this moment, the rest of us finally realized what had taken place and cracked up. We all laughed for about five minutes.

Ralph, like the rest of us, had no idea that Vinnie didn't have any professional experience performing in public and had never played anywhere other than in his basement at home.

Another funny story about Vinnie involved his first professional concert performance in front of a very large audience at the Equestrian Center in Prince George's County, Maryland. Because it was a big show with lots of big name acts, we had been practicing hard for this particular concert. Vinnie, however, had been practicing even harder than the rest of us. I had been messing with him about the upcoming concert by saying little things, such as, "Vinnie, don't forget that we're opening the show, and the first thing that the audience will hear is you playing the opening notes to our song, so you can't mess up." Vinnie doubled his efforts, and we all knew he would be ready for the show, but we didn't tell him that.

On the evening of the show, we were in our dressing room talking about the show, our music, and all the other routine stuff we usually do before performing. We all knew that Vinnie was nervous, and some of us attempted to ease his mind about going onstage. To make matters worse for Vinnie, he had invited a large group of people from the Navy Yard where he worked during the day to come see his first professional performance. And come they did. They occupied a whole section in the audience with big signs that said, "Go Vinnie." In addition, we had let Vinnie know that a lot of super groups from the fifties and sixties, such as Pookie Hudson and the Spaniels, the Orioles, the Dubs, the Five Discs, the Jewels, and the Capris, were also on the show with us. Ronnie, realizing that Vinnie was suffering from a bad case of nerves, took him aside and had him take a large gulp of an unknown liquid from his flask. It seemed to work or so we thought at the time.

Just before we were to go onstage, I asked one of the guys where Vinnie was, and no one seemed to know. I began to worry that he might have just said to hell with it and left the arena. I told all the guys to start looking for him because it was less than a half hour before we went on, and I needed him to be close.

After a short search, we finally found him. He was backstage, standing behind the curtain in the dark with an iron grip on his guitar, ready to go! We eventually pried he guitar out of his hands and got him back to the dressing room.

To Vinnie's credit, he performed that night like he had been doing it for years and like the pro he turned out to be. Vinnie stayed with the Memories until he retired from the United States Postal Service, a job he took after leaving the Navy Yard, and moved with his beautiful wife, Margie, to Williamsburg, Virginia. But before he left our group, Margie had the opportunity to see him perform at the Vocal Group Hall of Fame induction concert. Vinnie will always have a special place in both my heart and that of the Memories.

Chapter 72

The Capri's Incident: A Failure to Communicate

At this particular concert, we were sharing a dressing room with the Capri's of "There's a Moon Out Tonight" fame. Everything seemed to be going smoothly between both groups. I had established a warm relationship with the Capri's lead singer, Nick Santo, who was a really nice guy who also happened to be a retired police officer. He had retired from the New York City force, and I had retired from the Washington, DC, force.

We had been sitting around talking, and both Ronnie and Boots were busy doing whatever they usually do to get ready for our performance. After a short time we left the dressing room, which was located one level up from the stage, and we were walking toward the stage area when we heard one of the Capri's calling to us. He approached us and blurted out, "You guys can't sing 'Unchained Melody' with your show." The three of us were totally confused, and we asked him to explain what he was talking about. He flatly said that we could not sing that song during our performance, because they were going to sing the same song in their show. We obviously could tell that he was talking down to us. Both his tone and demeanor were very unfriendly, to say the least.

We told him that the promoter had specifically asked us to do that particular song during our performance. If he wanted it changed, he would have to speak to Wilbur Fletcher, the promoter of the show, about it. He continued to berate us and argued about how the Memories had a band and easily could change our song list, and that we were just being arbitrary about it. He was getting louder and began to demand that we agree not to do that particular song. I started to get ticked off and let him know where he could stick his demands. He pointed his finger at my chest and continued to tell us what to do. I kind of lost it and had just taken a step toward him with the intention of doing something stupid, when Boots grabbed me from behind and dragged me away from the confrontation, while I continued to tell the gentleman what I thought about him. Right away, I located the show's promoter and told him about the scene that had just occurred between me and one of the Capri's singers. Wilbur told me, "Don't worry about it. Just do your show the way you set it up and I'll take care of it." I felt pretty good about our conversation and was leaving the room when he said, "Make sure you don't take 'Unchained Melody' out of your show." I nodded and left.

On my way back to my dressing room, I saw Diz Russell of The Orioles and told him about the confrontation. What he said to me after hearing the story made me laugh so hard that tears came to my eyes. Diz said, "Louie, did they write 'Unchained Melody'?" I said no. He then asked, "Are you guys performing before they do?" I confirmed that we were. Diz looked at me, paused for a moment, and in a loud voice said, "To hell with them." I have often thought about what Diz said to me that night, and it still makes me laugh. It was priceless!

I went backstage, gathered our group together, and brought them up to speed as to what the promoter had said to me. We were all upset about the way the Capri's singer had acted and decided to go out there and play the hell out of that song. When our act was called, we went out and performed "Unchained Melody" better than we had ever performed it. In fact, we performed it so well that the audience gave us a standing ovation. Right after our show, the Capri's came out to do their show, and they also performed the song. There turned out to be two major differences between their performance and ours: their well-done rendition of "Unchained Melody" was entirely different than ours, and second, they didn't receive a standing ovation from the audience. I like to think that sometimes the good guys win!

Problems between performers do not happen often. In all my years as a performing artist, I can count on one hand the number of unpleasant incidents that have occurred between the Memories and other acts. Almost all the folks I've had the pleasure of working with throughout the years have been good, solid, hardworking people. There will always be exceptions to that rule, but that is what they are—exceptions.

Chapter 73

Robert Dove Jr.: An Injection of Youth

A few weeks after Vince "Vinnie" D'Orazio became a member of the Memories, and before we performed at the concert I previously mentioned, we added only the third drummer to ever play with our group. Tommy D'Pietro, our previous drummer, had retired after thirty years with our group, and we were left with the problem of finding a good drummer to replace him. What we needed was a drummer that not only played well, but one who also knew and understood our music. Boots Dove, one of our original members, suggested his son as a replacement for Tommy, and we began to entertain the idea that his son might work. As you might imagine, both Ronnie and I had known Rob Dove Jr. since he was born and had enjoyed watching him grow up.

When Rob Jr. was a teenager, he began to play drums in a group with some friends from his neighborhood. At one point, after some prodding from his dad, we hired Rob Jr.'s band to open for us at a gig we were doing for an automobile dealership in Clinton, Maryland. The kids were just teenagers, and we were all curious as to how well they would do. It was during the summer, and the gig was outdoors under a very hot sun. They did a good job, and although they needed a lot of work, they provided a very loud and enthusiastic opening for our show. Rob Jr. later told me that he thought they had done an outstanding job that day. Youth and confidence!

Over the ensuing years, Rob Jr. continued to play music with different groups and also began to write music. Along with the experience he acquired during his years of playing music, he also became an accomplished drummer. After discussing adding Rob Jr. to our group, we decided to give him a shot. Our rationale was not only did we need a new drummer but we also knew Rob, and it would be like adding a family member to our group. Rob Jr. became one of the Memories and brought with him an injection of youthful enthusiasm and excitement. Both Ronnie and I occasionally have to reign in his overly enthusiastic approach to our music, but to his credit, he has given us a ton of good ideas to improve our group performances along with his being a super drummer. He is also a lot of fun to be around!

Both Ronnie and I recently have begun helping him with his singing, and he is now singing lead on a couple of his dad's old tunes. In this case, the apple didn't fall far from the tree. Rob has been with us a good while now, and we expect him and his great personality to be with us to the bitter end. He remains both an important and fun part of our Memories family, as well as being a total team player.

Chapter 74

The Keyboard Man

Sometime after we let go our original keyboard man, we began to actively search for his replacement. A few months after our successful performance at the big doo-wop show in New York, it dawned on us that we desperately needed a keyboard player for several upcoming shows we had already contracted. Having upcoming gigs and no keyboard player really sucked. It just seemed to me that with us, it was always feast or famine. We needed to get help real fast!

What happened next proved that fate was in the mood to help us with our problem of not having a keyboard player. Ronnie had a day job as chief engineer for a big hotel chain, and one day while speaking with some of the women in the accounting office, who knew that he sang professionally, he casually mentioned that his group was looking for a keyboard player. Pam, one of the women in the accounting office said, "I know a keyboard player." Ronnie asked who it was, and she said her husband. Ronnie was excited and began to pepper Pam with questions regarding her husband and his musical background. Her husband, Charlie, had been playing professionally for a long time and had just recently decided to take a break from playing music. Ronnie asked her if she would talk to her husband and ask if he would be interested in playing music again. She said she would speak to him that evening about it.

Later in the week, Pam approached Ronnie and said that her husband had indicated that he wanted to see our group perform live. Ronnie gave

Pam the information about when and where they could come and see a group performance. It was early 2001 when Charlie and Pam came to see us perform at the Temple Hill Elks Club in Temple Hills, Maryland. I remember seeing a couple sitting at the band table that I was not familiar with. I also noticed that the guy appeared to be a quiet sort of person, and didn't seem to have much to say. When I later got to know him better, I realized that Charlie was one of those people who didn't talk unless he had something worth saying. Later in the evening, Ronnie told me that he was the keyboard player he had previously mentioned. A couple of weeks later I actually met Charlie Helmick at one of our practice sessions.

Charlie turned out to be a welcome addition to our group. The man's ability with the keyboards is amazing to both see and listen too. Right away, he began to add so much more music to our songs that Ronnie and I found ourselves shaking our heads in disbelief. He also had the ability to adapt very quickly to the different styles of music. Prior to joining the Memories, Charlie was used to playing mostly country music. Joining our group presented him with the large task of learning a whole new music genre. Charlie jumped in with both feet, and in no time, he seemed to have been playing our style of music all his life. He is that talented. He was also fortunate enough to have joined our group around the time we were being recognized by the Vocal Group Hall of Fame. As a result of that recognition, both Charlie and his wife Pam had the pleasure of visiting the hall of fame. Charlie also had the added bonus of having his wife see him perform with the Memories at the historic first induction concert of the Vocal Group Hall of Fame Museum. Since then, he has performed at several induction concerts for the hall of fame. Charlie has been with us for some time now, and even though he still doesn't talk a lot, his talent with the keyboard speaks volumes.

Chapter 75

The Vocal Group Hall of Fame & Museum

Beginning to describe one of the biggest events, if not the biggest event, to happen in the history of the Memories singing group is difficult. It all began in 1997, when Linda K. Stewart- Savach, the director of the Vocal Group Hall of Fame & Museum, contacted me and told me about the soon-to-be-opened Vocal Group Hall of Fame & Museum. She said they were considering our group for enshrinement. She said that she would be in further contact with me later in the process. She said that some other celebrity groups from the fifties and sixties had recommended the Memories. I later discovered that two of the groups who recommended our group for enshrinement were the Orioles and the Skyliners.

Chapter 76

Our Group Memorabilia

I was overwhelmed and quickly called Ronnie to tell him the big news about the hall of fame. This information equally blew him away, and he wanted to hear all the details. We discussed this life-changing news and decided not to pass it on to the others until we received further information. We didn't want to get any of the other guys prematurely excited by something that might or might not happen. Two months went by without a word. With every passing minute, I became more dejected. It seemed like just another heartbreak for our group.

I had just about given up hope of ever hearing from Linda K. Stewart-Savach again, when I received a phone call from a member of the hall of fame staff. I tried to hide my elation while listening to what they were telling me about their need for some Memories memorabilia for our museum case at the hall of fame. They also said that I would be receiving instructions by mail about how to send our memorabilia and how to fill out the affidavits that were necessary for the enshrinement process. I was so excited that I had them repeat the instructions three different times. They must have thought that I was mentally impaired by the way I was talking over the phone. I finally calmed down long enough to get the instructions straight before we hung up.

I again found myself waiting. I received the instructions from the hall of fame in about six or seven days. They sent the shipping labels for the boxes we would use to ship our stuff, along with lots of paperwork to fill out. We decided to ship some of our stage outfits; some early 45 rpm records by both the Memories and the Bobolinks; newspaper articles about us from nationally known news outlets; proclamations from state governors, state senators, and nationally recognized charities; show posters with our pictures; a pair of performance shoes worn by me onstage in the fifties; and group pictures depicting the group's performances around the country. We were also required to send photos of those stage outfits we had shipped, showing us actually wearing them while performing. We mailed everything away and settled in to await word. I was still skeptical about the whole situation even after sending and signing everything. We had endured so much heartache over the years that most of us had become somewhat cynical about the music business as well as some of the folks in it. We had been performing for almost five decades at that time, and we kind of thought that at the very least, our group deserved some recognition for the success we all felt we had earned. I hoped this was it. After several more weeks, I became anxious to know what was going on and decided to call Linda K. Stewart- Savach. She wanted to know when we would be coming to Pennsylvania to visit the Vocal Group Hall of Fame & Museum because she needed to arrange the press coverage for our visit. I told her that I would get right back to her with the date of our visit.

I immediately called everyone in the group, and most of us decided on a date for our visit. That's right, I said most of us. Even with the Memories receiving the greatest honor of our professional career, a couple of the guys in our group either couldn't, or wouldn't, take the time to go with us to visit our case. Those who did go were Ronnie Lutz, Glenn Bortz, Boots Dove, Tommy DiPietro, and me. I had a bitter taste in my mouth because a couple of people in our group chose not to be a part of something so important to all of us. Those group members, who chose to go, decided to not let the other group members' absence affect our trip to see if our dream had really come true.

When I called to confirm the dates of our visit to the museum, Linda K. Steward- Savach seemed genuinely pleased that we were coming and extended an invitation to our spouses to attend as well. She said that she would arrange for the press and a videographer to record our visit on video to be there when we arrived. She also gave me the instructions to the hotel where we would stay. Although we felt pretty special, a part of me was still a bit skeptical. Trying to explain how we all felt during our trip is difficult. I was so afraid that when we arrived at the museum that it would turn out to be a house trailer with a big sign on the roof. I never let on to the other guys what I was thinking or how nervous I was. I was just hoping that it would turn out alright in the end. Talk about a leap of faith!

When we arrived at the hotel, a hotel staff member greeted us and treated us like international stars. The hardest part for me and the other guys was acting like this kind of treatment was a normal occurrence for our group. We were in a very nice hotel within a mile of the museum. We could all feel the excitement in the air. Our visit was scheduled for the next day, and we decided to take the extra time to visit the nearby town of Sharon, Pennsylvania, to give our wives some shopping time.

While we were out and about in Sharon, we just couldn't resist the opportunity to drive by the museum. Wow! I was so relieved to see a big, beautiful building that took up the whole block. I was off the hook; it wasn't just a trailer with a sign on top. I really wanted to get inside that building to experience, what was for me, the realization of my biggest dream. The rest of that day was kind of hazy for me because all I could think about was what was going to happen the next day when we visited the museum to see our own museum case.

All of us met in the hotel dining room for breakfast the next morning. I could hardly eat because I was so excited. I think the other guys felt the same way I did. We sat around the breakfast table, making small talk for a short time , before we finally left for our long-anticipated visit to the Vocal Group Hall of Fame Museum.

Chapter 77

The Visit

Ronnie and I were very quiet during the drive to the museum. In fact, the only conversation inside the car was between our wives Sandy and Jinny. I imagine that the cars carrying the other guys were just as quiet. We were all just too nervous to talk. When our group walked up to the museum doors, we all stopped and stared at the building for a few minutes. Right about then, a man with a big camera on his shoulder approached us and introduced himself as the videographer who would be videotaping our visit for TV Channel Four News. He indicated that the museum director and some local reporters were waiting for us inside the building. We started feeling like we were someone special all over again.

We entered the museum's foyer while being filmed and walked to the front desk where several people were waiting for us. The museum director, Linda K. Stewart- Savach welcomed us. We introduced ourselves to her and the group of reporters. She then gave us ceremonial coins to put into the coin box for admission to the hall. She later gave all the Memories several of the coins for keepsakes and told us that she would be mailing us video copies of our visit. That video of our first visit to the Hall of Fame Museum can be seen in a movie about the Memories released in 2010 by MAE Productions, entitled *Dreams Come True*.

After we deposited our coins in the coin box, we went into the museum and were immediately impressed with just how beautiful the inside was. The building's interior design was truly elegant, and it appeared that no

Lou Martin

expense was spared in decorating it. We were jumping with excitement to see our museum case and had just started to walk up the beautiful wide staircase to where our display case was located, when the videographer stopped us and asked us to return to the first floor and start over so that he could get additional video of us climbing the stairs to see our case. We went along with it even though we didn't want to.

Chapter 78

The Memories Museum Case

We went up the stairs for the second time where staff members then guided us toward the Memories museum case. About ten feet from our case, we all suddenly stopped and stared at the beautiful case that displayed what amounted to a huge part of our lives. None of us had planned to stop where we did; we just did it at the same exact moment. I was stunned. I never thought that I would have such a reaction to our museum case. I was so overwhelmed that I started to tear up and had trouble catching my breath. Looking back on the experience, I realized that the other guys were having a similar reaction. I really don't know how to honestly express how I was feeling at that exact moment, other than to say, proud. I was prodded back to reality when the reporters asked us to get closer to our case. We moved right in front of the case and saw exactly what part of the Memories history was on display.

The museum staff had done a magnificent job of displaying the memorabilia that we had sent to them. The display was beautifully lit, and they even had mannequins, wearing our stage outfits. The neatest aspect was the interactive music button on the outside of our case that played portions of our early recorded songs when pushed. We all just stood there and took it all in. No one said a word for several minutes. Then a reporter started to ask questions about our group that momentarily took our minds away from the display case. Ronnie or I answered most of the reporters' questions because we were the two people who usually spoke for the group. At that point, the only thing the other guys wanted to do was to just look at our case.

Looking back on that first visit, the one thing that stands out the most for me was the look on the faces of the other guys when we all moved up close to our display case. From my perspective, the look on their faces took me back to 1957 when our original five teenagers started singing together on a street corner in southeast Washington, DC. In that moment, I was filled with both sadness and a huge sense of happiness at the same time. I really don't know how to explain that statement except to say that at that very moment, I remembered both the heartaches and setbacks we had suffered during our many years of performing along with some of the good times too. Saying that I felt like crying and laughing at the same time may sound a bit crazy, but that's the way I felt, as I stood in front of our beautiful display case at the museum.

The rest of the afternoon became a blur of answering questions, posing for pictures, and visiting the many other display cases of early rock-and-roll artists. After seeing the display cases of some of the other acts in the museum, we all felt that we were in pretty darn good company. Later that day, Linda K. Stewart- Savach indicated that she would be in touch with me to arrange for the Memories to perform at the upcoming Vocal Group Hall of Fame's induction concert. It just seemed to get better and better for us.

On the evening we returned home from our trip to the museum, I was lying in bed, trying to fall asleep and having no success. I turned to my wife Sandy and asked, "How in the hell did we manage to get into the hall of fame?" My amazing wife simply said, "Don't ask questions; just enjoy it." After I said my prayers of thanks, I went right to sleep.

Chapter 79

The Hall of Fame Concert

Several weeks later Linda K. Stewart- Savach contacted me to discuss our participation in the hall's first induction concert. At the time, I had no idea just how big this event was going to be. She informed me that the Memories were going to be part of the outdoor concert to be held right after the induction ceremonies inside the hall. She then asked if we would be available to perform on the date they had selected. Of course, I said yes. She then proceeded to tell me that the museum would provide our groups lodging and all transportation to and from our hotel and the museum. Furthermore, she said that they would take care of all press releases concerning the Memories participation at the concert.

After the phone conversation, I had a lot of work to do, such as making sure the date of the concert would work with the personal schedules of the other group members. Coordinating the schedules of eight people and their wives, who also have everyday lives to lead, isn't always easy. Despite having to figure out everything, I was smiling as I began the task of contacting everyone in our group to make sure the concert date at the hall of fame would work for them all. Our lead guitar player and longtime member of our group, who was still with us at the time, unfortunately stated that he couldn't make it. He was the same person who earlier had chosen not to go with the rest of us when we went to see our case in the museum the first time.

This presented a potentially serious problem for us because without a lead guitar player, we couldn't perform at the induction concert. I was really ticked off about the whole situation because this same person was again putting obstacles in the way of our group being able to continue to do the things we needed to do to achieve recognition and respect within our industry. I was left with the formidable task of finding a lead guitar player who was both good, and familiar with our music. After scratching my head and trying to think of who might fill the requirements for this important gig, I discussed the problem with my brother Denny, a former member of the Memories, who recommended a guy, Dave Panza, who occasionally played music with his current band, Avenue Grand Band. I knew of Dave from his reputation in the local music community and immediately thought that he could fit our immediate need for a lead guitar player.

After speaking with Ronnie, I contacted Dave about sitting in with our group on the date in question. He said that it sounded good to him, but that because of other commitments earlier in the day on the day of the concert, he wouldn't be able to travel up to the hall of fame with our group. He said he would meet us at the hall of fame later in the afternoon in time for our show. I wasn't very happy, because I'm a person who doesn't like surprises while performing. I'm almost fanatical about everything that happens during our performances being set in stone before going onstage. As I said, I don't like surprises, and this situation with Dave seemed loaded with surprises for us. I was really concerned that he would not make it to the hall in time to rehearse with us before the show. However because of the time constraints involved, we had no alternative but to go with Dave and we were stuck with our decision. I shouldn't have worried as much as I did, because Dave showed up in time to go over some of the tunes scheduled for our show and seemed to have a good grasp on both the various songs and how we wanted them to be played. He also seemed to be rather impressed with both the Vocal Group Hall of Fame Museum and the Memories museum display case.

I really can't describe the excitement of being around so many other high profile artists of the fifties, sixties, and seventies, who were scheduled to perform with us at the induction concert. We were flying high. The previous evening, we had the honor of being present at a dinner for all the other acts that would perform at the concert, and we were in awe of the nationally known performers sitting all around us. Sitting at our table was none other than Mary Wilson of the Supremes. Bill Pinkney and Charlie Thomas of the Drifters and Harvey Fuqua of the Moonglows sat at the next table. We were in some mighty fine company. Our wives were also enjoying the festivities, and both my wife Sandy, and Mary Wilson, seemed to strike up a genuine friendship over dinner and spent most of the evening in conversation. We had a ball.

On the following evening, after Tony Buttala of the Letterman introduced us, we went onstage and performed our show before thousands of hall of fame fans. To say that we were excited would have been an understatement. Dave, who didn't have a lot of practice time with us before our show, did an outstanding job as the replacement for our lead guitar player who didn't make the trip. That whole weekend of the induction concert was a dream for us all because it allowed us to perform with many of our musical idols.

Chapter 80

Johnny Angel and the Halos

Another special thing that occurred on that weekend was the opportunity to meet another performer who would later turn out to be both a personal friend to me and a friend to the Memories. His name is Jack Hunt, and I knew right away that we would become good friends. Jack, a talented singer and songwriter, had done a fantastic job of building an interactive display in the museum that truly represented street corner harmony groups. His group, Johnny Angel and the Halos, enjoyed tremendous popularity in the Pittsburgh area and also had performed at the induction concert that evening.

Some months later, the Memories had the distinct pleasure of both watching Jack perform, as well as performing with Jack and his fabulous group. Both Jack and I later became sitting members of the Vocal Group Hall of Fame & Museum Board of Directors as members of the induction committee, positions that we held from 1999 to 2001. We were both honored to do so. Later I was appointed by Linda K. Stewart-Savach to represent the Vocal Group Hall of Fame as a member of the National Music Museum Consortium Committee. This group met at various locations around the country to discuss ways to enhance the business prospects of the member museums, such as The Rock and Roll Hall of Fame, The Fender Guitar Hall of Fame, and so on. It proved to be an educational experience for me and a great way to meet other music industry people.

Chapter 81

The Hall of Fame Ring

*L*ater, after my appointment to the induction committee and while attending one of our board meetings, Tony Buttala, the board chairman, began to discuss what type of award the acts should receive upon their induction to the Vocal Group Hall of Fame Museum. He expressed the idea of a statuette he felt depicted both musical history and the museum. I didn't really like the idea at the time. I thought a ring like the one Super Bowl players get might be appropriate. Tony was not keen on the idea, so I dropped the idea for the moment.

Tony is the co-founder of the Hall of Fame with James Winner, so it was his absolute right to have the last word in the matter. I hoped that I could later change his mind. I later met with Linda K. Stewart- Savach, the director of the hall of fame at the time, and discussed my idea with her about the ring. She showed a lot of interest and authorized me to design a ring. I jumped at the chance to design the ring because I already had some ideas in my head and hoped to someday be lucky enough to receive one for myself and the other guys in the Memories. Color me selfish.

When I returned home from the board meeting, I started to design the ring. I had an idea what the ring would look like, but I hadn't yet put anything down on paper. I spent nearly two weeks perfecting the design so that it would reflect the hall of fame logo, the location of the hall, the year the act was inducted into the hall of fame, and assorted musical notes to surround the ring sides. I forwarded copies of the design to the hall and received encouraging feedback from Linda. After a few days had passed, I spoke with her and she agreed with the idea to have a prototype of the ring made (at no expense to the hall) and present it at the next board meeting for approval.

On the day of the next board of directors meeting, after the board discussed its usual routine business matters, the board adjourned for lunch. During lunch, I passed the prototype of the ring around the table and received favorable reviews from almost everyone at the table. The governor of Pennsylvania was at this particular lunch meeting and he also seemed impressed with the ring. At that time, I decided to back off pushing the ring because Tony had not expressed any interest in it. I honestly think that he rightfully wanted to use his idea of the statuette. Upon returning to the hall, I spoke with Linda who suggested I wait awhile and then present the idea to the board again.

Several months later, Tony again vetoed the idea because he felt that the cost to manufacture the number of 14 karat rings annually would be prohibitive. After thinking about his position and the budgetary concerns, I agreed with him and the other board members. We were left with the existing hall of fame rings, and no mandate to manufacture more. Linda then suggested that the rings stay with the Memories, because from that point on, new acts inducted into the museum would receive the statuette. The many musical icons enshrined in the Vocal Group Hall of Fame have warmly received the statuette envisioned by Tony.

Chapter 82

The Chordettes

The Memories were fortunate enough over the ensuring years to perform at several of the Vocal Group Hall of Fame concerts. Although they were all memorable and exciting, one concert personally proved to be even more exciting. The year was 2001, and our group had just walked into the Radisson Hotel lobby to register at the front desk, when we noticed a woman standing in the registration line in front of us with an older woman. We were talking when the young woman turned to us and said, "Are you here for the concert?" We all replied, "Yes we are." She responded, "I'm here with my mom for the concert. She's a member of the Chordettes." We all introduced ourselves and enjoyed some discussion about the upcoming concert that evening. After checking in, we pulled our cars around to the side parking lot to unload our luggage to take to our rooms. We were all pretty tired from the long trip and wanted to get to our rooms as quickly as possible. I had just entered the side hallway leading to the stairs, when the woman from Chordettes whom I had just met in the lobby stopped me and asked, "Aren't you one of the performers doing the show tonight?" I confirmed that I was. She went on to say, "Hello, I'm Jinny, and I'm with the Chordettes. We're on the show tonight too." She then added, "We haven't sung together for more than thirty years, and we need a pitch pipe. Do you have one?" I told her that I didn't have one, but I would try and find one for her.

Ronnie and I looked all over for a pitch pipe for her, but to no avail. I checked with other musicians and singers who were on the show that night, but we couldn't find a pitch pipe anywhere. We went back and told her that we were unable to find one. She was clearly disappointed and said, "I don't think we're going to be able to perform tonight unless I can find a pitch pipe." Both Ronnie and I offered to have our guitar player rehearse with them so that they could get ready for the show. She graciously thanked us for our efforts but declined the offer. She then left to tell the other women in the Chordettes about the problem.

I went back to my room to start getting ready for the induction concert. I completely forgot about finding a pitch pipe and spent the remainder of the afternoon making sure everything was in order for our evening show. After a small snack, we all went over to the concert area where we were shown our dressing room and the easiest way to get to the stage. We also made sure the wives were comfortably seated in the audience before we went back to the dressing room. After that, we just waited for our name to be called to go onstage and perform. When doing the bigger shows, waiting is always the hardest part.

We eventually went onstage and performed our show, which went smoothly. The large audience responded with lots of applause for our show. We went back to the dressing room, changed to our street clothes, and quietly joined the wives in the audience to enjoy the rest of the show. Watching from the audience while the other performers do their show and supporting them with my applause has always been a big thrill for me. I was able to enjoy the remaining acts that evening. One thing bothered me though, I never saw The Chordettes perform that evening. I was kind of busy, so I put it out of my mind for the moment.

After the show, all the performers were invited back to the Radisson Hotel lounge to relax and enjoy one another's company. The hotel had conveniently roped off the entrance to the lounge to prevent anyone, other than the performers, from gaining access. This posed a problem because I had invited my mother and my brother David and his wife Cathy to come to the concert to watch me perform, and I wanted them to be able to go into the lounge after the show to relax and enjoy meeting the celebrities. I spoke with a couple of the other performers who had family members with them, so I brought in my family, and it all worked out fine.

When we arrived at the lounge, it was a madhouse of people and performers mingling and having a good time. We were seated and had just received our drinks when Mary Wilson approached our table and began talking with us about the show. I later drifted away and sat down with Reese Palmer of the Orioles and Harvey Fuqua of the Moonglows, and we began to sing together. Ronnie came over to the table and began to sing along with us. Why do performers, who have just left the stage after performing, still want to sing when thrown together socially? My answer is simple: we love to sing!

About this time, Mary Wilson approached me and put a book into my hand. I asked, "What's this?" She said, "It's my book, and I want you to sign it." I was taken aback and hesitated for a moment before asking her, "Why would you want me to sign your book? She said, "I want all the talented artists that I perform with to sign this personal copy of my book, so just sign it." I was very flattered and humbled by her request, and I happily signed her book. Later, upon reflecting on that evening's festivities and my signing of Mary's book, I felt very proud.

Chapter 83

The Chordettes Private Performance

The room was full of musicians and performers who were having a great time.. I could just sense that this particular night was going to be magical. Tony Butala of the Lettermen had just finished pouring me a glass of wine from his bottle when I heard female voices singing from somewhere in the lounge. The whole room suddenly began to get quiet, and people were turning to look in the direction of the singing. I looked over and saw that the singing was coming from a table in the back corner of the lounge, which was occupied by several older women. I recognized one of the women as Jinny Janis of The Chordettes, whom I had spoken with earlier in the day about the pitch pipe. They were singing their hit record, "Mister Sandman" from the 1950s. At that moment, I realized that the other women sitting with Jinny must be the other original Chordettes. Maybe the reason they hadn't performed at the concert earlier was because we couldn't find a pitch pipe to help them rehearse for the show. I hoped not!

At that exact moment, almost everyone in the lounge got up from their seats and began to make their way over to the Chordettes' table. I joined everyone and did a double take, because sitting with the Chordettes was my son, Lou Martin Jr., who had just played in the hall of fame golf tournament that afternoon. Knowing my son and his personality, I wasn't really surprised that he would be sitting with the Chordettes. They seemed to be enjoying his company, and they later told me what a great guy he is.

I just stood there and listened to these women who sounded like they had never stopped singing together. I was honestly amazed at how good they sounded. They actually sounded just like their record, and almost everyone standing around their table had their cell phones out in an effort to capture this magical moment. The other performers wanted their friends and loved ones to share this special moment too. The sad part of this story is that my mom, who had watched me perform at the concert earlier in the evening and who was a big Chordettes fan, had decided to go up to her room to rest. When she later found out what she had missed, she was crushed.

The gathering of artists that night proved to be one of the most fun and rewarding nights in the Memories history. Months later, while talking with several of the artists who had been in the lounge on the evening when the Chordettes had sung, I realized that I wasn't the only one who thought that particular evening had been magical. The special feeling generated in the lounge that evening has for me never been duplicated. I feel sad that what we were privileged to see and hear that night will never be repeated in my lifetime. Since that time, one of the original Chordettes has passed away. Now their special sound can only be carried in the hearts and minds of those who knew and loved them. I'm one of those people!

Chapter 84

Harvey Fuqua: The Moonglows

Earlier that same evening, my son, Lou Jr. first met Harvey Fuqua of the Moonglows when he was standing near the stage while the show was going on, and became engaged in a general conversation with both Harvey and his wife who were also standing close to the stage. At the time, my son had no idea who Harvey was or what he did for a living. While he was talking with Harvey, our group came onstage and began our performance. My son later told me that he pointed out to Harvey that the guy singing lead was his dad, and he asked Harvey "Do you think he still has it?" Harvey replied, "I don't think he ever lost it." After the show, I walked over to the three of them, and Harvey told me about his conversation with my son. He also said, "Man, I meant every word of it; you guys did a great job." What a great compliment from a fellow performing artist and a doo-wop and R&B legend.

Speaking of my son, Lou Jr., any recollection I have about the Memories hall of fame experience must include him. Over a period of several months, Lou Jr. became very close to both Tony Buttala and Jim Winner, co-founders of the Vocal Group Hall of Fame & Museum. He spent a lot of time with both of those gentlemen working on solutions to many vexing problems facing the hall at that time. Not only did he give of his time to help the hall, he also gave financial support to the hall of fame. For example, for their celebrity golf tournament and dinner, he donated more than $30,000 worth of sports memorabilia to be auctioned off to benefit the hall of fame. Not a lot of people knew about it, and I think Lou Jr. wanted it that way. Jim thought so highly of him that later he worked with Lou Jr. on a couple of business deals. I'm proud to say that all of my children have been supportive of my singing career and seem to be proud of their dad's accomplishments. I'm right tickled about that!

Chapter 85

Mary Wilson of the Supremes: How I Became a Member of the Supremes

Performing together with artists like Mary Wilson at the Vocal Group Hall of Fame & Museum were great times for us and the various artists who were enshrined in the museum and also for the staff of the fledging museum. Everyone seemed to be enthusiastic about the hall of fame and the excitement that it generated within the music community.

For us performing artists, the Vocal Group Hall of Fame & Museum seemed to be the only place in a long time where the artists and their body of work became the center of focus. I, along with the other members of our group, had the opportunity to mix with so many famous artists of the fifties and sixties at the hall that it seemed like a musical Disneyland to us all. From this experience, I had the pleasure of getting to know Mary Wilson as a fellow performing artist and friend.

The Memories had been invited to perform at the Vocal Group Hall of Fame induction concert in 2002, but because of other commitments, most of our group members couldn't make it in time to perform. We sadly declined the invitation to perform, and I notified the hall of our inability to be a part of the show. However, Tony Buttala of the Lettermen and co-founder of the Hall of Fame invited me to the show as a VIP guest. I accepted his invitation and made arrangements to attend.

Because of the large demand for tickets to the show, the induction concert was held in a semi-pro baseball stadium in nearby Ohio. I was backstage, having a blast hanging out with some of the performing artists who were getting ready to go out and do their show, when Mary Wilson approached me and asked if I could help her with a big problem she was having. Of course, I said yes. She took me aside and explained that her backup singers couldn't make it to the show, and she was scheduled to perform in about one hour. She described how her manager had found two local singers to stand in for her regular backup singers.

I was more than a little confused by the conversation we were having and finally asked her "How can I help you?" She explained that after working with both women on the songs, she realized that neither one of them could sing harmony.

Both of the young women were lead singers in local bands and had never learned to sing harmony. Mary was scheduled to do her show in about an hour and she needed the girls to be ready to back her up onstage. In other word she needed them to sing harmony. Again I asked, "How can I help?" Mary then asked me to accompany her to where the women were waiting and work with them on their harmony parts. I told her I would give it a try.

After meeting the two women, I discussed the songs Mary would be singing in her show and the vocal parts the two women would need to learn. I told them that they needed to learn their parts pretty quickly because Mary's show was now only forty minutes away. I began to work with them on their individual harmony parts to the two songs Mary would be doing in her show. After working with them for almost thirty minutes, I began to panic. Neither woman seemed to have any knowledge of how to sing harmony nor could they keep from continuously crossing over and singing each other's notes. We were in deep trouble.

Mary, who had been coming into the room every ten minutes or so to check on our progress, again walked into the room and asked how it was going. I took her outside in the hallway and told her the bad news. She was a bit upset by this information and said she didn't know what she was going to do about her show. She then asked me if I would go onstage with her and the two female vocalists and sing with them. I told Mary that I hadn't brought any stage clothes with me and only had the suit I was wearing. She said it was fine for onstage. She was grasping at straws at the time and didn't really want to be a part of a disaster in the making. I told her that I would only do her show if the women would agree to an idea I had. I explained that because the two women seemed to only know how to sing lead vocals, I would have them both sing the same note and I would sing the harmony note.

Mary thought it was a great idea! I left her, went into the rehearsal room, and sold the idea to the two women. We went over the two songs a couple of times before showtime. While walking to the stage, I took a minute to also work out how we would be physically moving while singing. I had noticed during our rehearsal that the women seemed to have exaggerated hip movements while singing.

Because I was a guy and thankfully didn't have the same type of hip movement, I asked them to tone it down a little so we all would appear to be in sync while onstage. They both laughed and agreed to hold back. I also laughed, and it seemed to help them settle down a bit before going onstage. Backstage, we could look out from behind the curtains and see that the stadium was sold out, which seemed to make the women nervous. They had never performed in front of such a large audience before, and it seemed to unnerve them, which didn't make me happy.

I told them they should think of the audience without clothes, and it would help them get through their performance. I like to think that in a small way that my advice helped them get through the show.

Chapter 86

Show Time: Mary Wilson and Charlie Thomas

The stage manager called Mary's name, and we walked out onto the stage in front of Mary and took our position behind our microphones just before she came out. I whispered to the girls to concentrate and not to forget to kick off on their left foot, so that we would move in sync. The music started, and Mary started to sing. Our vocals seemed to work very well, and the girls stayed on their one note throughout the whole performance. They did a really good job!

About halfway through her show, Mary stopped the band, walked over to me, introduced me to the audience as being one of the Memories, and introduced me as being her first male member of The Supremes. The crowd loved it, and I did too! Mary finished her show, and after taking her last bow, she began to leave the stage. We began to fall in behind her to leave the stage, when Charlie Thomas of The Drifters, who was just off stage, yelled at me, "Lou, stay there, I need you guys to back me up." We went back to our original positions behind our microphones, and I told the women, who were now in a panic, not to worry about it, but to just "sing what I sing." I knew that Charlie was only going to sing one song, "Under the Boardwalk," and the background for the song was very simple.

Unbeknownst to the women, I was sweating bullets. I knew we hadn't rehearsed this song, and they had no idea what the background vocals required. I turned to them and whispered "Under the Boardwalk and they looked at me like I was crazy. I whispered "Under the Boardwalk" a second time, and they again gave me a bewildered look. At this point, while Charlie was talking to the audience, I seized the moment to whisper that the background vocal line was simply a repeat of the lead line "under the boardwalk" sung by Charlie.

Once again I told the women to watch me and do what I do. They followed my lead, and the whole thing turned out pretty good. I was very proud of them and told them so. I also invited them to stay backstage and mingle with the other artists after the show. They were thrilled! Truthfully speaking, I had no real authority to invite them to stay, but I did it anyway, and they seemed to really enjoy being around all the singing legends from the fifties and sixties.

Chapter 87

The Flamingos

Over the years the Memories have enjoyed performing with many of the groups who were household names during the magical fifties and sixties. Not only did we perform with them, we were also fortunate enough to claim many of them as our friends. One of the byproducts of working with other artists was that we personally got to know them and developed some great friendships.

One group of performers who we worked with numerous times was the highly regarded superstar group, the Flamingos. The Memories weren't the headliner act of those gigs we shared with the Flamingos, but they always showed us respect and treated us like equals. That's the kind of guys they were. I remember a funny incident that occurred when both of our groups were booked to perform at the same concert.

It was during the mid-1990s, and a promoter contacted us and asked if we would be interested in performing with the Flamingos at a Chesapeake Bay beach concert. The date was acceptable to us, and we agreed to do the gig. The nice thing about this particular gig was that it was reasonably close to home and didn't require any lengthy travel for most of the guys in our group. Not only did we get to perform with some really nice guys, but we also would be able to go home and sleep in our own beds.

On the day of the show, we arrived at the concert venue at the beach and were directed to the dressing room, where we hung our show outfits in the space provided. Up to this point in time, we had not seen any of the

Flamingos nor did we notice any of their clothing in the dressing rooms. We went about our business to make sure the band equipment was being set up properly and ensuring we were ready for our sound check scheduled for a little later in the afternoon.

Everything went smoothly during the sound check. When the Flamingos arrived, we had enough time before the show to sit around and catch up with them on the latest news and gossip. Because we were going on first, followed by a short intermission between our acts, the Flamingos had not spent any time in our shared dressing room.

A few minutes before we were to go on, we were dressing, when J.C. Carey and Larry Jordon of the Flamingos came into the dressing room to wish us good luck. Up until that moment, we hadn't given much thought to the outfits we had chosen for that particular concert. When J.C. and Larry saw what we were wearing, they just busted up laughing.

We had forgotten that the Flamingos group color was pink, the same color as the pink flamingo bird. It suddenly dawned on us that our stage outfits were flamingo pink in color. Here we were, doing a show with a tremendously popular group like the Flamingos, and we were wearing the colors associated with their act. We were so embarrassed! We immediately offered to take the jackets off and do our show without them, but both Larry and J.C., who were still laughing, said no way and that they would borrow them when we finished with our show.

We went out and performed our show with several of the Flamingos sitting in the back of the hall laughing their buns off. They were great sports about the whole situation, and we still enjoy a good laugh about it whenever we see each other. They are truly a super nice group of guys and always a lot of fun to perform with.

Chapter 88

Mike Scheer

Just before Ralph McDuffie, our original saxophone player, retired in 2006 from the Memories, both Ronnie and I spoke to him about who he might recommend to replace him. Ralph said that he would think about it and let us know at the next practice. At the next practice, Ronnie and I again asked him, and Ralph said he could not think of many sax players who could play our kind of music the right way, and he could only think of one, Mike Scheer, who might fit into our group structure and fit our group's musical needs.

Both Ronnie and I knew Mike from watching him perform with other acts over the years, mostly with the Avenue Grand Band. We had enjoyed hearing Mike play on numerous occasions in the past. We knew about his ability to play a terrific saxophone, so we never had any question about his talent. I'm a guy who hates change. I had become so used to Ralph's easygoing demeanor and his willingness to do whatever we needed him to do, that I felt that we couldn't find anyone else who would fit as smoothly into our group structure. I thought that finding someone who could fill Ralph's shoes would be really hard.

Before Ralph left for Florida, I again told him of my misgivings. What he said made a lot of sense. Ralph said, "Lou, everybody plays sax differently, and Mike will do a good job for you guys." I began to realize that despite my reservations about a new sax man, change might be good for our group after all.

We contacted Mike and talked to him about joining our group. Mike liked the idea, but he indicated that he was involved with another group part time and had to discuss it with that group. Our only concern at that time was what would happen if we had a booking that conflicted with the other group. Mike assured us that he could work it out with the other group because they weren't performing very often. Ronnie and I decided to ask Mike to join the Memories even though I felt that he might have a problem playing in a structured environment like ours. Everything we do onstage is highly structured, which means that every musician knows exactly what to play and when to play it on every song. No more, no less.

Mike had in the past usually played with groups that allowed him a lot of leeway to improvise his saxophone leads. From my point of view, he is the kind of sax player who has been very successful during his long career by playing a freestyle saxophone. That became a concern to us, because we were a group who had gained our reputation by attempting to faithfully perform oldies tunes almost exactly the way they were originally done. We talked with Mike about our concerns regarding this matter, and he assured us that it wouldn't be a problem. I believed Mike would be able to adapt to the musical changes required to fit into the Memories family because he was so talented. Even so, being the worrying type, I still harbored slight reservations about our newest member. My worries proved to be misplaced.

Mike brought with him a wealth of experience and innovative ideas that the Memories could utilize in future performances. He also brought with him an almost ritualistic routine he would go through before each and every performance. Ronnie and I would crack up just watching him prepare before he would go onstage. First, he would remove his sax from its case, place it on its stand, and take a minute or two to look around. Next, he would pull out his reed container, taking lots of time to look at his assortment of reeds. Only then would he pick out the one he would be using for that particular performance. Next, he would take a couple of minutes to look around. At this point, he would go through an elaborate routine of licking the reed, placing it in a glass of water, and then after a few more minutes, placing the reed in the reed holder. He would then blow the sax a couple of times and then pull the reed out and go through the whole process all over again. We would all get a big kick out of watching the performance before his actual performance. We started calling him "lightning" because it took him so much time. Over his long career, all that preparation has paid off for him. It's called, "being professional"! What an interesting guy.

Mike has been with the Memories family for a long while now, and we feel very fortunate to have him with us onstage. He has probably forgot more about playing saxophone than most of the current crop of sax players will ever know about playing their instrument. He has also brought us the added pleasure of the company of his lovely wife, Marge, who accompanies Mike to most of our gigs.

Chapter 89

Neil Arena

I have written about how most of our group members initially joined our group team. Most people have no idea how vocal groups or bands are actually formed or how they change members. In our case, the change to our group began in 2006 when Robert "Boots" Dove, our original baritone and friend of more than fifty-five years, was forced to retire because of ill health. His retirement really sent us into a tailspin, because after singing harmony with him for so many years, we couldn't envision our group sound without him providing the baritone part we had grown so accustomed to. We immediately started searching around for someone to take Boots's place in the baritone spot. We again found ourselves in a familiar position—locating a seasoned professional singer who knows how to sing harmony parts.

During a phone call to a friend of mine, Danny Bruno, a talented singer and song writer who lived in Daytona Beach, Florida, I discussed our search for a replacement baritone for our group. Danny and I had written a couple of songs together, and we had become close friends as a result of our shared love of music. As I talked about our dilemma with him, he said he would start spreading the word and be on the lookout for someone who might fit into our group. I didn't have much hope that he would find anyone because he was living in Florida at the time, and I doubted he could find a replacement in Florida for a group in Maryland.

A couple months later, I received a phone call from Danny telling me that he has someone in mind who might fit into our group, a guy by the name of Neil Arena. What he said next really got my attention. Danny told me that this guy, Neil, was the original baritone for the Mellow Kings. I knew right away who the Mellow Kings were, because they had enjoyed a number one hit with a song called, "Tonight, Tonight." I remembered singing along with this song many times while daydreaming about my own group, the Bobolinks, making it big like the Mellow Kings had. I told Danny that we were interested. I told him to have Neil give me a call so that we could discuss our mutual interest. I was also curious as to how Danny had found Neil.

Danny told me that recently one of the guys in his vocal group, Dennis, had called him and wanted him to meet his friend, Neil Arena from New York, who was visiting Florida at the time. During the meet and greet, Danny learned about Neil's music background with the Mellow Kings. Danny told Neil about our group, the Memories, and related some of our musical history. He also told him about the conversation he had with me regarding our search for a baritone to replace Boots. Neil told him that he was very interested in our group and would like to talk to me about joining the Memories. Furthermore, he explained that he was living in northern Virginia, which was not very far from where our group was based. Danny gave Neil my phone number and told him to give me a call. The rest, as they say, is history.

A couple of weeks later, I received a call from Neil. We exchanged pleasantries and then began the process of exchanging information about his musical history, experience, and so on. I also learned that he was Italian American, which clinched the deal for me, because I'm also Italian American and a bit partial to other Italian Americans. During the conversation, Neil sounded both friendly and very positive about joining our group. He related to me his history with the Mellow Kings and mentioned he had not been singing regularly for several years. He seemed eager to audition, and we agreed on a date and location for the audition. At this time, the Memories had been rehearsing for about a year in Arlington, Virginia, in the hotel where Ronnie worked as chief engineer. This proved to be a good location for Neil, because he didn't live far away.

At the audition, Neil met the rest of the guys in the group, and we proceeded to outline the songs we were going to do. Neil knew most of them, which made us happy. Neil was a typical New Yorker, gregarious and very sure of himself. The boy could sing, but we realized right away that it would take a lot of hard work on our part to teach him our harmonies and song formats for all the songs we performed in our shows. We decided to bring Neil on board. Neil worked hard to learn our material and showed definite signs of the professional he had been in the early days of his career with the Mellow Kings. Everyone liked Neil, and he brought a new energy to the group.

A few months after Neil joined the Memories, Ronnie and I began to see signs of a lack of attention on Neil's part along with his inability to retain a memory of his harmony parts. Unbeknown to the rest of us in the group, Neil had been going through a private hell of his own. When I asked Neil about his mistakes in the harmony and his lack of attention during practice, he took me aside and explained to me that his loving wife of many years was dying from cancer, which explained everything. The worst part was the only thing we could do was to offer our support to Neil. This sad situation took many months to play out. To his credit, Neil still insisted on attending rehearsals, even though we knew his heart was breaking.

After his wife died, Neil slowly came back to being the guy we all came to know in the beginning of our relationship. He began to sing the way we had hoped he would, and he also came up with ideas about choreography for the singers on certain songs. We loved it! Neil continued to progress as time went along. He was also instrumental in obtaining gigs for our group, which was very important to the Memories. We began to go on the road a lot, performing in different states, for a variety of events and organizations. Neil continued to do well, although he seemed to have problems with doing anything physical, such as moving band equipment or lifting anything heavy.

After asking Neil about it, he told me that he had bad knees and back problems. He also said he had heart problems, which precluded his doing any heavy physical exertion. About this time, Ronnie and I began to worry about Neil being able to continue with the Memories over the long haul. To his credit, he would, from time to time, attempt to help with the band equipment.

The Memories continued to perform with Neil until July, 2011 when Neil's health became an immediate concern to both Ronnie and me. At the time, our group was performing in West Virginia for a Fourth of July celebration. On that particular day, we had two shows scheduled in two different towns at two different times. The temperature was in the high nineties, and both shows were to be performed outdoors. It was really hot and even hotter onstage in our show clothes. We had an air-conditioned dressing room, but the minute we stepped outside, we began sweating heavily. We all noticed that Neil was suffering a lot more than the rest of us. After our first show, his stage outfit was completely soaked through and he looked really tired and pale. Neil had even rested his hand on my shoulder for some support during the show, something he had never done before. He was such a professional that he made it look like part of the show. When we got ready to go onstage for the second show, Neil was in pain and still so exhausted from the first show that Ronnie had to help him up the stairs to the stage. We both began to really worry about Neil having a heart attack or worse while onstage performing. The main reason we were concerned was, that after this second show, we had to immediately leave for another town forty-five miles away to perform another two shows in this same terrible heat.

Ronnie and I talked about it with Neil. Being the professional he is, he said he was all right and wanted to continue to perform. We successfully completed the second set of shows, and although it was still hot, the heat subsided because of a little rain and approaching darkness. As far as both Ronnie and I were concerned, this scare with Neil made both of us face the fact that we would need to start thinking about replacing Neil because of his health issues.

Chapter 90

The Reluctant Decision

I n addition to Neil's health issues, we also had to discuss with him his continued insistence on taking a three- to four-month vacation in Florida during the winter months. We had no argument with his desire to stay warm during the winter, but we had a serious problem with the length of his vacation. By simply being away from the group for this long period of time, he denied our group the viability of aggressively looking for work for one quarter of the year. No professional group can stay inactive for that period of time and expect to stay relevant in show business. On several occasions, I personally discussed my concerns with Neil about how it would affect our ability to get work during his absence. His response was, "We don't have anything scheduled for those months anyway." I tried to point out to him that with his vacation already planned, we couldn't schedule any gigs, even if they were offered to us. He also seemed to not believe me when I told him if he continued with his plans to be away for the winter months, we would have to make other arrangements.

After serious discussions about the issue, we decided that it would be in both Neil's best interest and that of the Memories for him to retire. We really felt bad about this because we all really liked and respected Neil and his large talent. During his five years with the Memories, he added much needed personality and energy to our group. We all miss the New York accent along with his great sense of humor.

And so the search began anew for a replacement vocalist for our group. It was never easy, and we didn't think it would be easy this time around either. We were all getting older, so it became imperative that we find someone to fit our group mold, and quickly return to the studio to finish the new album that we had started in 2011. Getting back to performing as soon as possible was also equally important to us.

Chapter 91

Rick Williamson

The group had known for some time that Vinnie was going to retire from his job, and he and his wife would soon be moving away from the area. That meant we would have to begin our search for a new lead guitar player right away if we were going to be able to maintain our gig schedule. Replacing a musician to perform in an oldies band isn't easy. We found ourselves in the same position again. Ronnie and I began to rack our brains about who we could find to replace our current guitar player. The crop of available, and more importantly, dependable lead guitar players was exceedingly thin. We faced several problems. First, the music business was in real bad shape because of the economy. Secondly, the enforcement of drunk-driving laws, which caused a severe loss of revenue (because people elected to stay home and drink), resulted in club owners and other venues steering away from live bands in favor of disc jockeys. A DJ can never replace a live band, although a DJ is cheaper.

After a few weeks, neither Ronnie nor I had come up with a solution. Then one day, a couple of months before Neal left the group, Ronnie invited my wife and me over for a backyard cookout. While in Ronnie's back yard, we started discussing the problem we were having finding a lead guitar player. Ronnie mentioned that one of his guests was a guitar player named Rick Williamson. After a few minutes of wandering around the yard saying my hellos, I sat down with my wife, Sandy, across the table from a couple whom we had not met before. We introduced ourselves and began to talk with them about the trivial things that go along with people meeting for the first time. Sometime during our conversation, we started talking about music, and I discovered that Rick was the guitar player Ronnie had been telling me about. He was also one of Ronnie's neighbors.

Rick seemed to be a very nice guy and appeared to be interested to hear that the Memories were looking for a lead guitar player. He mentioned to me that he hadn't played professionally for a long time, and that he had, for the most part, played mostly classic rock before putting down the guitar. About this time, Ronnie joined us, and he and I were immediately on the same page. We asked Rick if he would like to play with the Memories. Rick said, "I haven't played in a long time, but let me think about it." While he was thinking about it, he took the time to come and see us perform in concert at Reston, Virginia. He must have liked what he saw and heard, because after thinking about it, he called Ronnie and said he would like to be part of our group, which turned out to be a good decision for both the Memories and Rick.

He became our newest member. I began to get to know the new guy and attempted to find out what his playing abilities were. I was also not completely sure that his personality would fit with our group. I needn't have worried, because Rick not only brought a great work ethic to our group, but he also brought along his dry sense of humor to entertain us. He fell easily into the group scheme, and his personality and enthusiasm soon won over the group skeptics.

He is the kind of guy that you want to work with because he is willing to do the hard work necessary to do the job. Rick began to learn our music, and although he was quite rusty in the beginning, he was soon up to speed with our group repertoire. After he began to get comfortable with our set lists, he started to flesh out his guitar leads, and I began to hear some interesting lead notes coming from his guitar. We loved it!

Another interesting thing about Rick is that when we decide to learn a new song, we never have to worry about his not knowing the song when we first rehearse it. That's because we know that he will have done his homework and worked hard to practice the songs and be ready to play. One more thing that both Ronnie and I like about Rick is that he is always willing to do extra work with the vocalists whenever we need him to be there. He also has the added blessing of being married to a terrific woman named Linda who has also become a big part of our group family.

Chapter 92

Our "Special Memories"

I'm going to take a moment and say something about a very special group of women who have supported both our music as well as each group member individually. I'm speaking about the wives of our band members. They have always been there to support us with their presence, and occasionally, even their labor. They are solely responsible for us looking decent while on stage. They make sure that our stage outfits are always ready to go. They even go on the road with us while we do what we do. On the rare occasions, when our regular road sales crew (Judy and George Shaffier) couldn't make it, the wives have pitched in and successfully handled the sale of our Memories merchandise. They share our dream, and we couldn't do it without them. My personal gratitude goes out to all of you.

Chapter 93

June Flynn

Our vocal group has always consisted of only male performers. This was not a conscious effort to exclude women, but the result of almost all vocal groups of the fifties being comprised of only male singers. Because those examples were all that our group had to pattern ourselves after, we followed suit. The composition of all male singers in our group seemed to work out very well for us until 2011. While our group was on the road performing, Ronnie and I thought of replacing Neil, who was having health problems and decided to discuss the matter with him when we returned from the road trip.

In the meantime, we faced the oncoming reality of being one person short in the vocal harmony portion of our group. Because we were obligated by contract for several upcoming performances, we needed to find a replacement as quickly as possible, which isn't easy to do for a few reasons. First, we have to find someone who could sing on a professional level. Secondly, we had to find someone who could sing harmony. Being able to sing harmony is one of the hardest parts of being a trained vocalist. In addition, we needed someone to know the type of music that our group performs. In other words, the person has to, more or less fit with our age group and is able to sing the songs from our era the right way. From a social point, this person had to fit in with the other band members.

The change in our group lineup began while we were performing in Ocean City, Maryland, for a police convention. During one of the band breaks I spoke with our sax man, Mike Scheer. Mike approached me to discuss the question of whether we were going to replace Neil with another singer anytime soon. I told him that because of Neil's health issues, we had to consider it. Mike then said, "I know a really good singer I've played with for many years, who might be interested in singing with our group." I asked who that person might be, and he said her name was June Flynn. I was taken aback for a moment, but I asked Mike more about June. He gave her a glowing recommendation for her singing ability and her stage presence. He further stated that she was very good with lead vocals as well as harmonies.

When he mentioned her ability to sing harmony, I began to listen more closely to what he was saying. I asked a few more questions about her and then told him that I would get back to him after Ronnie and I had the opportunity to discuss the matter. After the gig, while driving home, Ronnie and I discussed the whole idea of bringing a girl into the group. Having been in the music business for so many years, we understood the pitfalls involved with having a woman in an all-male performing group, especially while performing on the road.

One of the problems we would face with having a female in the group was getting the promoters to provide an additional hotel room for our group as well as a separate dressing room for her. This extra accommodation translated into money, and promoters are not in the business of giving any more money to performers than they have to. Finally, and most important, we wanted to make sure that the band members' wives would approve of this person. If the wives didn't like her, this new addition to our group wouldn't happen.

I called Mike, got June's phone number, and called her to set up a meeting at Ronnie's house for the following week. I had never met June before, and I don't think that Ronnie had either, so we had no preconceived ideas about her prior to our meeting with her. Before our meeting with June, Ronnie and I had, on numerous occasions, talked about what it would mean to us and to the rest of the group to have a female in our group. Ronnie was very positive about the situation. I was a little less so. Anyway, we decided that this was another opportunity for our group to reinvent ourselves once again. We also decided that having a female would give us a new energy along with the ability for our group to do a lot of new songs that feature a female lead singer. It would also give the Memories a new look and new sound.

When we first met June, it felt as if we had all known each other a long time. She had a delightful personality along with an unassuming persona. We spent a good part of the first meeting discussing what each of us expected to get out of our new association together. She was easy to talk to and not at all pushy. Had she been pushy, the meeting would not have lasted very long. I wasn't being chauvinistic; it was just me again resisting change. We didn't do much in the way of singing at our first meeting, but we did pretty much sort out the role Ronnie and I had envisioned for her to play within the group.

Ronnie and I decided that June would be a great addition to the Memories, so we set up the next practice session only for group vocals. Prior to singing with the Memories, June had been accustomed to singing more leads with her old group, Redstone. Our group's needs at this time dictated that in the beginning, she should concentrate on her background harmonies until she could master enough of our show songs to enable her to perform at our upcoming concerts. She quickly showed us that she had the chops to sing almost anything we asked of her. She quickly learned the song lyrics and musical arrangements. Ronnie and I assured June that we would begin work on lead vocals for her as soon as we fulfilled our upcoming performance obligations, and we followed through on our promise.

The first meeting that brought June face to face with the other band members' wives occurred at my house one summer afternoon at a poolside practice session. I was nervous about the wives liking June and treating her cordially. I shouldn't have been nervous because June won them over with her wonderful personality and self-deprecation. They all liked her. It was now safe to go forward because we had the band wives' seal of approval.

June's first public performance with the Memories occurred on October 1, 2011 in Myrtle Beach, South Carolina. She came onstage and performed like the professional she certainly is. Not only did she sing her parts on time and on key, but she also moved in sync with Ronnie and me while performing the various songs in our show. That's not an easy thing to do. She added a huge amount of energy and personality to the show, and we loved it. June has continued to impress her fellow band members with her work ethic and her willingness to go the extra mile for our performances. We all look forward to many performances with June at our side.

Chapter 94

FAME: Friends Against Musical Exploitation

Back in the late nineties, I had occasion to meet an individual who would later become a good friend to me and many other musical artists around the country. What brought us together was the Vocal Group Hall of Fame & Museum. We both ended up on the hall of fame induction committee together, and as a result of that meeting and our shared love of music, we became good friends.

A chance remark about the exploitation of musical group's identities on my part started the conversation between Pat Benti and me. The matter had been personal to me for quite some time, because I discovered that other groups were using the Memories name to illegally promote themselves. We, as a group, have been using this name since 1961 and legally own (copyrights) for both the name and logo. This didn't seem to deter many groups from using our name to promote themselves in different venues around the country. They seem to have no shame! We had to spend money to have our attorney send cease-and-desist letters to those groups who were unlawfully using our name.

What really got me steamed about the situation was the Memories have been working hard for many years to promote our group name. We have endured a lot of hardships over the years while working to make a name for ourselves, only to find out that some Johnny-come-lately groups have come along and illegally appropriated our name for their own use. These bums have not earned the right to use our name, and if they had an ounce of integrity, they would cease using our group name immediately. I have learned that it's not a perfect world.

I found out that Pat also felt strongly about the issue of people stealing the hard-earned names of groups who have spent years of hard work building their group identity. He told me that he had started an organization to address this particular issue. He then began to tell me the story about Friends against Musical Exploitation (FAME) and how it came to be.

Chapter 95

The Beginning of FAME

P at Benti started FAME in Boston in1998 and became executive director, along with Gene Hughes of the Casinos and Dennis Yost of the Classic Four.

Mary Wilson of the Supremes and Herb Reed of the Platters later joined them. Because Pat was acquainted with Brian O'Conner, who was the administrative assistant to Congressman Joseph Kennedy, he arranged a trip to Washington, DC, to lobby various members of Congress about the unlawful use of legitimate groups names and logos. He also contacted other well-known performing artists, such as Carl Gardner of the Coasters, Charlie Thomas of the Drifters, Joe Terry and Frank Maffei of Danny & the Jrs, and Chuck Blasko of the Vogues, to accompany him to lobby Congress about their concerns.

Many musical celebrities made several lobbying visits over the ensuing years in an attempt to draw attention to this serious issue of musical identity theft. I also had the honor of being a part of this lobbying effort and was interviewed on television about our group's personal experiences regarding the illegal use of our name by others.

Pat later related an unusual story about one of his visits to a congressman's office to lobby about our issue. He and his entourage had the unfortunate occasion to visit Rep. Barney Frank's office the day after his live-in male friend had a run-in with the press, which subsequently caused the public outing of Rep. Frank. Pat told me that their visit to the office had not been very productive, because of the sensational publicity surrounding Rep. Frank's personal dilemma that required his attention.

FAME kept plodding along until ABC television's *Primetime* aired an interview with Carl Gardner, Chuck Blasko, and Dennis Yost about the unlawful use of celebrity group names by people posing as the original artists. That interview along with several articles in *Goldmine* Magazine started the ball rolling in a big way. Since then, several laws have been enacted against the unlawful use of another group's professional identity. It took a long time, but thankfully, it finally happened. Pat is still going strong with his musical performances throughout the northeast. He specializes in Italian-American shows, which receive amazing responses from the Italian community in his hometown of Boston, Massachusetts.

Chapter 96

Sacrifice

The success we accomplished as a group was worth both the emotional and physical price each of us had to pay over the years. Most people only see the musicians and singers performing their specialty and naturally don't think about how it all came to be. That's normally the case where crowds gather to be entertained by these performers. What they don't know, and have no need to know, is just how much each individual singer or musician has had to give up for the privilege of entertaining them.

For the Bobolinks/Memories, the sacrifice translated into rehearsing our music six and seven days a week. In the beginning, we just enjoyed being together and singing. We were all young, and none of us was married at that time. We were having so much fun that, at times, we lost sight of what we were trying to accomplish. Buddy, our manager at the time, quickly refocused us to rehearsing the songs we were supposed to be learning. As a result of hundreds of hours of practice time, we became vocally tight. That is to say, our harmonies were super. I often think back on the hundreds of practice sessions we attended over the years we've been together, and if I were to guess, overall, we probably put in more than a hundred thousand hours of practice time. That time translated into time away from our family and friends. I'm not complaining because I believe that our good Lord picked this path for me and wanted me and the guys to bring a little bit of happiness to each of our fans, by taking them back to a happy place in time when a particular song meant something special to them

Later, as we gained notoriety, we were more or less forced to continue rehearsing long hours to stay sharp for all the singing jobs we were starting to receive. Along with learning new material to perform, several of the guys were in serious relationships and considering marriage. As you might expect, that situation forced us to make adjustments to our practice schedule, which was the beginning of many changes in the way we operated as a group. It wasn't all bad, just different. We were used to being together a lot, and after a couple of our guys got married, we began to change.

Time passed, and most of the guys were married with children. We again attempted to change our patterns to accommodate the married guys. We continued occasionally going on the road to perform, but our travel was reduced a bit to accommodate the guys with families. Even after trying to adjust practice and performing times so as not to conflict with family activities, there were casualties. Over the ensuing years, after much time away from their spouses and children, several of our group members suffered divorces. We all knew what we were giving up, but we thought that what we might accomplish in the end justified our sacrifices. It took an awful lot of years and an awful lot of tears for that to happen.

Having said all that, I would bet that if asked, most musicians and singers would say that given a choice, they would elect to do the exact same thing all over again. You've got to love what you do!

Chapter 97

Sacrifice II

Traveling can sometimes be a real chore. Musicians who travel to the various show locations to perform can attest to that. When arriving at a gig, performers usually check into the hotel, hook up with the promoter, and then get ready for the sound check. Any actively performing band member can attest to the many hours spent just waiting around for the sound man to set the sound levels for their group's performance. It's a time-consuming process, because all the acts have to get their sound levels set at the sound check, which means waiting for their turn. After the sound check, performers basically hang around and kill time until the performance. It can be lonely and seriously boring.

Over the many years I spent with our group, I was very selfish with the time I allocated to rehearsing and performing that resulted in time away from my family. Hindsight is always better than foresight. Most of the guys in the group, at one time or another, and in varying degrees, suffered some regret over this same issue. That part of being in a professional singing group is not often talked about and is not very glamorous. Another part of being a singer is the constant worry about your singing voice and how to protect it from the elements. Singers always worry about catching colds or anything else that might affect their singing performance. They become paranoid about keeping their throat safe, so they always carry lozenges or anything else to get them through the show. For me, it seems to have worked pretty well over the years. I can only remember one performance in fifty-five years that I couldn't make because of throat problems. I've been blessed!

We all gave up a lot to be able to do what we loved to do. For most of the Memories, after investing so much of our lives in our music, it turned out pretty amazing. All of us have been able to enjoy the recognition and success.

Chapter 98

And the Beat Goes On

I never honestly thought that I would have so much to say about the Memories history. From having lived these very personal experiences, I just assumed that others might not enjoy reading my personal recollections about the pursuit of young men's dreams. I hope to be proven wrong.

This is the beginning of the Memories fifty-sixth year of performing, and we still enjoy not only the performing part, but also the fellowship that comes from a group of people being together for such a long period of time, doing something they love and were born to do.

I can't say that the long hours of practice necessary to prepare for a performance have become easier over the years. They haven't. If anything, the long hours seem to have become somewhat harder. I often find myself questioning the relevance of our music in today's musical environment. It somehow seems so yesterday. I guess that's probably the main reason the Memories have enjoyed the amazing success we've been able to sustain over these many years. Perhaps I should do less thinking about the miserable state of the current music scene and more about just enjoying our group success.

These days our success seems to emanate from a shrinking, but still sizeable group of folks. These people have decided to enjoy their oldies and want to hear them played by an authentic doo-wop group who actually lived the songs. Because of our group's music history and maturity, our audience almost immediately seems to associate with us. It's funny how they react when we attempt to do more current songs. Our audiences quickly lets us know that they prefer what we do best—the oldies.

The Memories don't perform as much as we have in past years, but when we do perform, the gigs seem to be located in much better venues with better pay. Because the Memories history goes all the way back to the golden years of rock-and-roll and because of those musical credentials, we still get calls from promoters of the big oldies shows with offers to appear in concert with many other acts from the fifties and sixties. We really enjoy doing those shows, because of the opportunity to renew old show business friendships with other performers.

In this stage of our careers, we only take the gigs that both appeal to us as a group and offer us quality exposure to our audiences. We are still actively performing, recording, and learning new material. Our latest album will be released by MAE Productions in November, 2012. We haven't given up just yet! Please visit the Memories web site @ www.thememories.org. The Memories will keep on ticking. Stay with us because "The Beat goes on."

About the Author

LOU MARTIN SR. was born in 1938. He studied at American University and Pacific Western University, where he earned a bachelor's of science degree in the administration of justice. He is a retired law enforcement officer, former United States Congress staff investigator, poet, singer, and song writer. The father of three children and six grandchildren lives on the shore of the Chesapeake Bay in Maryland with his wife Sandra.

CPSIA information can be obtained at www.ICGtesting.com
Printed in the USA
LVOW11*2318161113

361580LV00002B/223/P